MICHELANGELO

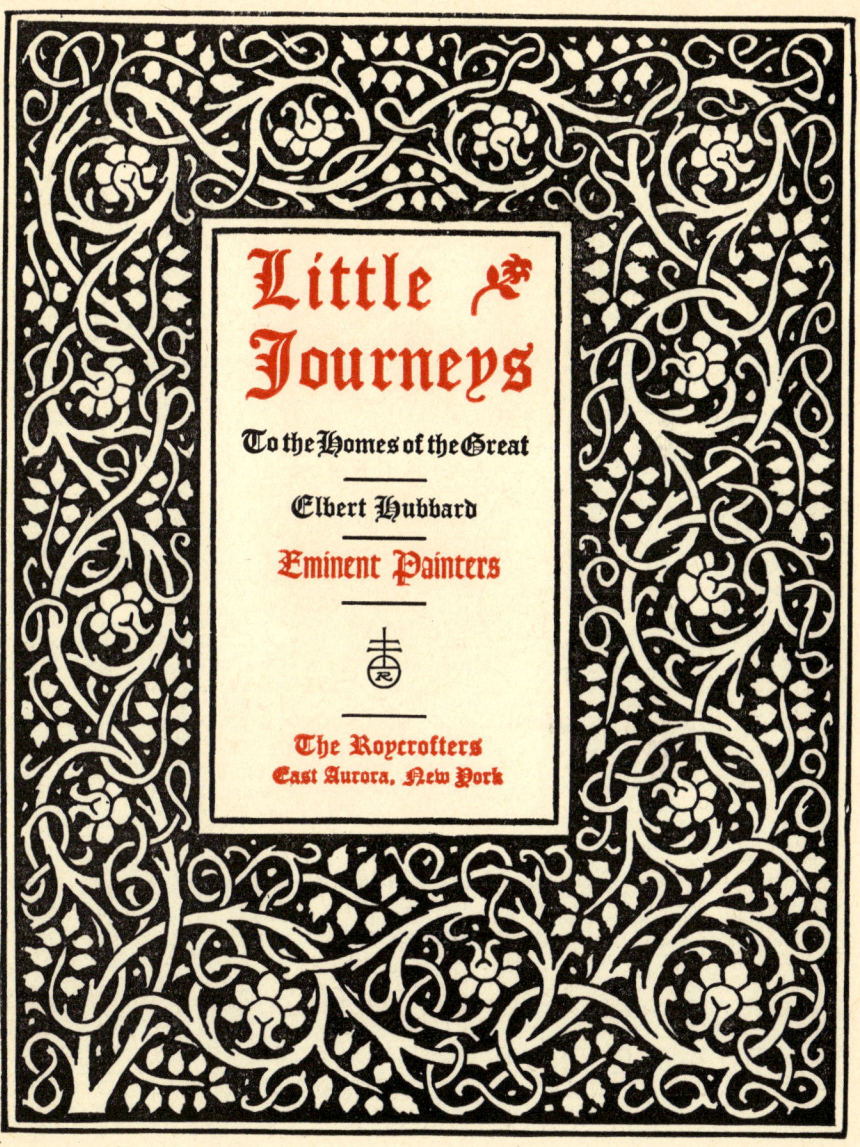

Copyright, 1928
By
The Roycrofters
(All Rights Reserved)

Manufactured in U. S. A.

CONTENTS

MICHELANGELO	3
REMBRANDT	39
RUBENS	79
MEISSONIER	117
TITIAN	145
ANTHONY VAN DYCK	171
FORTUNY	199
ARY SCHEFFER	223
FRANCOIS MILLET	257
JOSHUA REYNOLDS	285
LANDSEER	309
GUSTAVE DORE	327

Little Journeys
To the Homes
of
Eminent Painters

MICHELANGELO

How can that be, lady, which all men learn
By long experience? Shapes that seem alive,
Wrought in hard mountain marble, will survive
Their maker, whom the years to dust return!
Thus to effect, cause yields. Art hath her turn,
And triumphs over Nature. I, who strive with
    sculpture,
Know this well: her wonders live
In spite of time and death, those tyrants stern.
So I can give long life to both of us
In either way, by color or by stone,
Making the semblance of thy face and mine.
Centuries hence when both are buried,
Thus thy beauty and my sadness shall be shown,
And men shall say, "For her 't was wise to pine."
    —*Sonnets of Michelangelo*

MICHELANGELO

"ALL me by my pet name," wrote Elizabeth Barrett Browning, in one of those incomparable sonnets of which the Portuguese never heard. And the task yet remains for some psychologist to tell us why, when we wish to bestow the highest honor, coupled with familiar affection, we call the individual by a given name.
Young men and maidens will understand my allusion; and I hope this book will not suffer the dire fate of falling into the hands of any one who has forgotten the days of his youth.
In addressing the one we truly revere, we drop all prefix and titles. Soldiers marching under the banner of a beloved leader ever have for him a name of their own. What honor and trust were once compressed into the diminutive, "Little Corporal," or Kipling's "Bobs"; or, to come down to something even more familiar to us, say, "Old Abe" and "Little Phil"!
The earth is a vast graveyard where untold millions of men lie buried, but out of the myriads who pass into forgetfulness every decade, the race holds a few names embalmed in undying amber.
Lovers of art, the round world over, carry in their minds one character, so harmoniously developed on

MICHELANGELO

every side of his nature that we say twenty centuries have never produced his equal. We call him "Leonardo"—the one ideal man. Leonardo da Vinci was painter, poet, sculptor, architect, mathematician, politician, musician, man of science, and courtier. His disposition was so joyous, his manner so captivating, his form and countenance so beautiful, that wherever he went all things were his. And he was so well ballasted with brains, and so acute in judgment, that flattery spoiled him not. His untiring industry and transcendent talent brought him large sums of money, and he spent them like a king. So potent was his personality that wherever he made his home there naturally grew up around him a Court of Learning, and his pupils and followers were counted by the score. To the last of his long life he carried with him the bright, expectant animation of youth; and to all who knew him he was " Leonardo—the only Leonardo."

But great as was Leonardo, we call the time in which he lived, the age of Michelangelo.

When Leonardo was forty, and at the very height of his power, Michel Agnola Buonarroti, aged twenty, liberated from the block a marble Cupid that was so exquisite in its proportions that it passed for an antique, and men who looked upon it exclaimed, " Phidias! "

¶ Michel Agnola became Michelangelo, that is to say, " Michel the Angel," in a day. The name thrown at him by an unknown admirer stuck, and in his later

MICHELANGELO

years when all the world called him "Angelo" he cast off the name his parents had given him and accepted the affectionate pet name that clung like the love of woman ❧ ❧

Michelangelo was born in a shabby little village but a few miles from Florence. In another village near by was born Leonardo. "Great men never come singly," says Emerson. And yet Angelo and Leonardo exercised no influence upon each other that we can trace. The younger man never came under the spell of the older one, but moved straight on to his destiny, showing not the slightest arc in his orbit in deference to the great luminary of his time.

The handsome Leonardo was social: he loved women, and music, and festivals, and gorgeous attire, and magnificent equipage. His life was full of color and sweeping, joyous, rainbow tints.

Michelangelo was homely in feature, and the aspect of his countenance was mutilated by a crashing blow from a rival student's mallet that flattened his nose to his face. Torrigiano lives in history for this act alone, thus proving that there are more ways than one to gain immortality ❧ ❧

Angelo was proud, self-centered, independent, and he sometimes lashed the critics into a buzzing, bluebottle fury by his sarcastic speech. "He affronted polite society, conformed to no one's dictates, lived like an ascetic and worked like a packmule," says a contemporary.

MICHELANGELO

Vasari, who among his many other accomplishments seems to have been the Boswell of his time, compares Leonardo and Michelangelo. He says, " Angelo can do everything that Leonardo can, although he does it differently." Further, he adds, " Angelo is painter, sculptor, engineer, architect and poet." " But," adds this versatile Italian Samuel Pepys, somewhat sorrowfully, " he is not a gentleman."
It is to be regretted that Signor Vasari did not follow up his remarks with his definition of the term " gentleman." ⚜ ⚜
Leonardo was more of a painter than a sculptor. His pictures are full of rollicking mirth, and the smile on the faces of his women is handed down by imitation even to this day. The joyous freedom of animal life beckons from every Leonardo canvas; and the backgrounds fade off into fleecy clouds and shadowy, dreamy, opiate odor of violets.
Michelangelo, however, is true to his own life as Leonardo was to his—for at the last the artist only reproduces himself. He never painted a laugh, for life to him was serious and full of sober purpose. We can not call his work somber—it does not depress—for it carries with it a poise and a strength that is sufficient unto itself. It is all heroic, and there is in it a subtle quality that exorcises fear and bids care begone.
No man ever portrayed the human figure with the same fidelity that Angelo has. The naked Adam, when the

MICHELANGELO

finger of the Almighty touched him into life, gives one a thrill of health to look upon, even after these four hundred years have struggled to obliterate the lines.
¶ His figures of women shocked the artistic sense of his time, for instead of the Greek idealization of beauty he carved the swelling muscles and revealed the articulations of form as no artist before him had ever dared. His women are never young, foolish, timid girls—they are Amazons; and his men are the kind that lead nations out of captivity. The soft, the pretty, the yielding, were far from him. There is never a suggestion of taint or double meaning; all is frank, open, generous, honest and fearless. His figures are nude, but never naked ✣ ✣

He began his artistic work when fourteen years old, and he lived to be eighty-nine; and his years did not outlast his zeal and zest. He was above the medium size, an athlete in his lean and sinewy strength, and the whipcord quality of his body mirrored the silken strength of his will.

In his old age the King arose when Michelangelo entered the Council-Chamber, and would not sit until he was seated at the right hand of the throne; the Pope would not allow him to kneel before him; when he walked through the streets of Rome the people removed their hats as he passed; and today we who gaze upon his work in the Eternal City stand uncovered.

MICHELANGELO

ICHELANGELO was the firstborn in a large family. Simone Buonarroti, his father, belonged to an ebbtide branch of the nobility that had lost everything but the memory of great ancestors turned to dust. This father had ambitions for his boy; ambitions in the line of the army or a snug office under the wing of the State, where he might, by following closely the beck and nod of the prince in power, become a magistrate or a keeper of customs ✄ ✄

But no boy ever disappointed a proud father more.

When great men in gilt and gold braid, with scarlet sashes across their breasts, and dangling swords that clicked and clanged on the stone pavement, strode by, rusty, dusty little Michel refused to take off his cap and wish them "Long life and God's favor," as his father ordered. Instead, he hid behind his mother's gown and made faces. His father used to say he was about as homely as he could be without making faces, and if he did n't watch out he would get his face crooked some day and could n't get it back.

Simone Buonarroti had qualities very Micawber-like mixed in his clay, and the way he cringed and crawled may have had something to do with setting the son on the other tack.

The mother was only nineteen when Michel was born, and although the moralists talk much about woman's vanity and extravagance, the theory gets no backing

MICHELANGELO

from this quarter. She was a plain woman in appearance, quiet and self-contained, with no nerves to speak of, a sturdy, physical endowment, and commonsense enough for two. When scarcely out of dresses the boy began to draw pictures. He drew with charcoal on the walls, or with a stick in the sand, and shaped curious things out of mud in the gutters.

It was an age of creative art, and most of the work being in the churches the common people had their part in it. In fact, the common people were the artists. And when Simone Buonarroti found his twelve-year-old boy haunting the churches to watch the workmen, and also discovered that he was consorting with the youths who studied drawing in the atelier of Ghirlandajo, he was displeased.

Painters, to this erstwhile nobleman, were simply men in blue blouses who worked for low wages on high scaffolds, and occasionally spattered color on the good clothes of ladies and gentlemen who were beneath. He didn't really hate painters, he simply waived them; and to his mind there was no difference between an artisan and an artist.

The mother, however, took a secret pride in her boy's drawings, as mothers always do in a son's accomplishments. Doubtless she knew something of the art of decoration, too, for she had brothers who worked as day laborers on high scaffolds. Yet she didn't say much about it, for women then didn't have so much

MICHELANGELO

to say about anything as now. ¶ But I can imagine that this good woman, as she went daily to church to pray, the year before her first child was born, watched the work of the men on the scaffolds, and observed that day by day the pictures grew; and as she looked, the sun streamed through stained windows and revealed to her the miracles of form and color, and the impressions of "The Annunciation," "Mary's Visit to Elizabeth" and "The Babe in the Manger" filled her wondering soul with thoughts and feelings too great for speech. To his mother was Michelangelo indebted for his leaning toward art. His father opposed such a plebeian bent vigorously:
"Bah! to love beautiful things is all right, but to wish to devote all of one's time to making them, just for others—ouch! it hurts me to think of it!"
The mother was lenient and said, "But if our child can not be anything more than a painter—why, we must be content, and God willing, let us hope he will be a good one."
Ghirlandajo's was practically a school where, for a consideration, boys were taught the secrets of fresco. The master always had contracts of his own on hand and by using 'prentice talent made both ends meet. Young Michel made it his lounging-place and when he strayed from home his mother always knew where to find him ❧ ❧
The master looked upon him as a possible pupil, and

MICHELANGELO

instead of ordering him away, smiled indulgently and gave him tasks of mixing colors and making simple lines. And the boy showed such zest and comprehension that in a short time he could draw freehand with a confidence that set the brightest scholar in the background. Such a pupil, so alert, so willing, so anxious, is the joy of a teacher's heart. Ghirlandajo must have him —he would inspire the whole school!

So the master went to the father, but the father demurred, and his scruples were only overcome when Ghirlandajo offered to reverse the rule, and pay the father the sum that parents usually paid the master. A cash payment down caused pater to capitulate, and the boy went to work—aged fourteen.

The terms of his apprenticeship called for three years, but after he had been at work a year, the ability of the youth made such an impression on the master that he took him to Lorenzo, Lorenzo the Magnificent, who then ruled over Florence.

Lorenzo had him draw a few sketches, and he was admitted to the Academy. This "Academy" was situated in the palace of Lorenzo, and in the gardens was a rich collection of antique marbles: busts, columns, and valuable fragments that had come down from the days when Pericles did for Athens what Lorenzo was then doing for Florence. The march of commerce has overrun the garden, but in the Uffizi Gallery are to be seen today most of the curios that Lorenzo

MICHELANGELO

collected. ¶ By introducing the lad to Lorenzo, Ghirlandajo lost his best helper, but so unselfish was this excellent master that he seemed quite willing to forego his own profit that the boy might have the best possible advantages. And I never think of Ghirlandajo without mentally lifting my hat.

At the Academy, Michelangelo ceased to paint and draw, and devoted all his energies to modeling in clay. So intent was his application that in a few weeks he had mastered technicalities that took others years to comprehend ✄ ✄

One day the father came and found the boy in a blouse at work with mallet and chisel on a block of marble. "And is it a stone-mason you want to make of my heir and firstborn?" asked the fond father.

It was explained that there were stone-masons and stone-masons. A stone-mason of transcendent skill is a sculptor, just as a painter who can produce a beautiful picture is an artist.

Simone Buonarroti acknowledged he had never looked at it just in that way, but still he would not allow his son to remain at the trade unless—unless he himself had an office under the government.

Lorenzo gave him the desired office, and took the young stone-mason as one of the Medici family, and there the boy lived in the Palace, and Lorenzo acted toward him as though he were his son.

The favor with which he was treated excited the envy

MICHELANGELO

of some of the other pupils, and thus it was that in sudden wrath Torrigiano struck him that murderous blow with the mallet. Torrigiano paid for his fierce temper, not only by expulsion from the Academy, but by banishment from Florence.

Michelangelo was the brightest of the hundred young men who worked and studied at the Medici palace.

But when this head scholar was eighteen Lorenzo died. The son of Lorenzo continued his father's work in a feeble way, for Piero de Medici was a good example of the fact that great men seldom reproduce themselves after the flesh. Piero had about as much comprehension of the beautiful as the elder Buonarroti. He thought that all these young men who were being educated at the Academy would eventually be valuable adjuncts to the State, and as such it was a good scheme to give each a trade—besides, it kept them off the street; and then the work was amusing, a diversion to the nobility when time hung heavy.

Once there came a heavy snowstorm, and snow being an unusual thing in Florence, Piero called a lot of his friends together in the gardens, and summoning Michelangelo, ordered him to make a snow image for the amusement of the guests, just as Piero at other times had a dog jump through a hoop.

"What shall it be?" asked Michelangelo.

"Oh, anything you please," replied Piero; "only don't keep us waiting here in the cold all day!"

MICHELANGELO

Young Angelo cast one proud look of contempt toward the group and set to work making a statue. In ten minutes he had formed a satyr that bore such a close resemblance to Piero that the guests roared with laughter. "That will do," called Piero; "like Deity, you make things in your own image." Some of the company tossed silver coin at the young man, but he let the money lie where it fell.

Michel at this time was applying himself to the study of anatomy, and giving his attention to literature under the tutorship of the famous poet and scholar, Poliziano, who resided at the court.

So filled was the young man's mind with his work that he was blind to the discontent arising in the State. To the young, governments and institutions are imperishable. Piero by his selfish whims had been digging the grave of the Medici. From sovereignty they were flung into exile. The palace was sacked, the beautiful gardens destroyed, and Michelangelo, being regarded as one of the family, was obliged to flee for his life. He arrived in Bologna penniless and friendless, and applied to a sculptor for work. "What can you do?" the old sculptor asked. For answer, Michelangelo silently took a crayon and sketched a human hand on the wall. Marvelous were the lines! The master put his arms around the boy and kissed his cheek.

This new-found friend took him into his house, and placed him at his own table. Michelangelo was led into

MICHELANGELO

the library and workrooms, and told that all was his to use as he liked.

The two years he remained at Bologna were a great benefit to the young man. The close contact with cultured minds, and the encouragement he received, spurred his spirit to increased endeavor. It was here that he began that exquisite statue of a Cupid that passed for an antique, and found its way into the cabinet of the Duchess of Mantua.

Before long the discovery was made that the work was done by a young man only a little past twenty, and Cardinal San Giorgio sent a message inviting him to Rome ❧ ❧

MICHELANGELO

OME had long been the Mecca of the boy's ambitions, and he joyously accepted the invitation. At Rome he was lodged in the Vatican, and surrounded by that world of the beautiful, he went seriously about his life's work. The Church must have the credit for being the mother of modern art. Not only did she furnish the incentive, but she supplied the means. She gave security from the eternal grind of material wants and offered men undying fame as reward for noble effort.

The letter of religion was nothing to Michelangelo, but the eternal spirit of truth that broods over and beyond all forms and ceremonies touched his soul. His heart was filled with the poetry of pagan times. The gods of ancient Greece on high Olympus for him still sang and feasted, still lived and loved.

But to the art of the Church he devoted his time and talents. He considered himself a priest and servant to the cause of Christ.

Established at Rome in the palace of the Pope, Michelangelo felt secure. He knew his power. He knew he could do work that would for generations move men to tears, and in his prophetic soul was a feeling that his name would be inseparably linked with Rome. His wanderings and buffetings were things of the past—he was necessary to the Church, and his position was now secure and safe. The favor of princes lasts but for a day, but the Church is eternal. The Church should be

MICHELANGELO

his bride; to her and to her alone would he give his passionate soul. Thus mused Michelangelo, aged twenty-two. His first work at Rome was a statue of Bacchus, done it seems for an exercise to give Cardinal Giorgio a taste of his quality, just as he had drawn the human hand on the wall for his Bologna protector; for this fine and lofty pride in his power was a thing that clung to Michelangelo from rosy youth to hoary age.

The " Bacchus," which is now in the National Museum at Florence, added to his reputation; and the little world of art, whose orbit was the Vatican, anxiously awaited a more serious attempt, just as we crane our necks when the great violinist about to play awakens expectation by a few preliminary flourishes.

His first great work at Rome was the " Pieta." We see it today in Saint Peter's at the first chapel to the right as we enter, in a long row of commonplace marbles, in all its splendid beauty and strength. It represents the Mother of Christ, supporting in her arms the dead body just after it was lowered from the cross. In most of Michelangelo's work there is a heroic quality in the figures and a muscular strength that in a degree detracts from the spirit of sympathy that might otherwise come over us. It is admiration that seizes us, not sympathy. But this early work is the flower of Michelangelo's genius, round and full and complete. The later work may be different, but it is not better.

When this group was unveiled in Fourteen Hundred

MICHELANGELO

Ninety-eight it was the sensation of the year. Old and young, rich and poor, learned and unlearned, flocked to see it, and the impression it made was most profound. If the Catholic Church has figured on the influence of statuary and painting on the superstitious, as has been tauntingly said, she has reckoned well. The story of steadfast love and loyalty is masterly told in that first great work of Michelangelo. The artist himself often mingled with the crowds that surrounded his speaking marble, and the people who knelt before it assured him by their reverence that his hand had wrought well. And once he heard two able doctors disputing as to who the artist was. They were lavish in their praise, and one insisted that the work was done by the great sculptor at Bologna, and he named the master who had befriended Michelangelo. The artist stood by and heard the argument put forth that no mere youth could conceive such a work, much less execute it.
¶ That night he stole into the church and by the wan light of a lantern carved his name deep on the girdle of the Virgin, and there do we read it today. The pride of the artist, however, afterward took another turn, for he never thereafter placed his name on a piece. " My work is unlike any other—no lover of the beautiful can mistake it," he proudly said.

He worked away with untiring industry and the Church paid him well. But many of his pieces have been carried from Rome, and as they were not signed and scores of

MICHELANGELO

imitations sprang up, it can not always be determined now what is his work and what not. He toiled alone, and allowed no 'prentice hand to use the chisel, and unlike the sculptors of our day, did not work from a clay model, but fell upon the block direct. " I caught sight of Michelangelo at work, but could not approach for the shower of chips," writes a visitor at Rome in the year Fifteen Hundred One.

MICHELANGELO

ERFECT peace is what Michelangelo expected to find in the palace of the Pope. Later he came to know that life is unrest, and its passage at best a zigzag course, that only straightens to a direct line when viewed across the years. If a man does better work than his fellows he must pay the penalty. Personality is an offense.

In Rome there was a small army of painters and sculptors, each eager and anxious for the sole favor of the powers. They quibbled, quarreled, bribed, cajoled, and even fair women used their influence with cardinals and bishops in favor of this artist or that.

Michelangelo was never a favorite in society; simpering beauty peeked at him from behind feather fans and made jokes concerning his appearance. Yet Walter Pater thought he found evidence that at this time Michelangelo was beloved by a woman, and that the artist reproduced her face and form, and indirectly pictured her in poems. In feature she was as plain as he; but her mind matched his, and was of a cast too high and excellent to allow him to swerve from his high ideals. Yet the love ended unhappily, and in some mysterious way gave a tinge of melancholy and a secret spring of sorrow to the whole long life of the artist.

Jealous competitors made their influence felt. Michelangelo found his work relegated to corners and his supplies cut short.

At this time an invitation came from Florence for him

MICHELANGELO

to come and make use of a gigantic block of marble that had lain there at the city gate, blackening in the dirt, for a century.

The Florence that had banished him, now begged him to come back.

" Those who once leave Florence always sigh to return," says Dante. He returned, and at once began work on the " David." The result was the heroic statue that stood for three hundred years at the entrance to the Palazzo Vecchio, only a hundred feet from where Savonarola was hanged and burned. The " David " is now in the Belle d' Arte, and if the custodian will allow you to climb up on a ladder you will see that the top of the head shows the rough unfinished slab, just as it was taken from the quarry. Any one but a master would have finished the work.

This magnificent statue took nearly two years to complete. As a study of growing youth, boldly recognizing all that is awkward and immature, it has never ceased to cause wordy warfare to reign in the camp of the critics. " The feet, hands and head are all too large," the Athenians say. But linger around the " old swimmin'-hole " any summer day, and you will see tough, bony, muscular boys that might have served as a model for the " David."

The heads of statues made by the Greeks are small in proportion to the body. The " Gladiator " wears a Number Six hat, and the " Discobolus " one size

MICHELANGELO

smaller; yet the figures represent men weighing one hundred eighty pounds each. The Greeks aimed to satisfy the eye, and as the man is usually seen clothed, they reduced the size of the head when they showed the nude figure.

But Michelangelo was true to Nature, and the severest criticism ever brought against him is that he is absolutely loyal to truth. He was the first man ever to paint or model the slim, slender form of a child that has left its round baby shape behind and is shooting up like a lily-stalk. A nude, hardy boy six years old reveals ankle-bones, kneecap, sharp hips, ribs, collar-bone and shoulder-blade with startling fidelity. And why, being Nature's work, it is any less lovely than a condition of soft, cushioned adipose, we must let the critics tell, but Michelangelo thought it was n't.

From Fourteen Hundred Ninety-six, when Michelangelo first arrived in Rome, to Fifteen Hundred Four, he worked at nothing but sculpture. But now a change came over his restless spirit, for an invitation had come from the Gonfaloniere of Florence to decorate one of the rooms of the Town Hall, in competition with Leonardo da Vinci—the only Leonardo.

He painted that strong composition showing Florentine soldiers bathing in the Arno. The scene depicts the surprise of the warriors as a trumpet sounds, calling them to battle with the enemy that is near at hand. The subject was chosen because it gave opportunity for

MICHELANGELO

exploiting the artist's marvelous knowledge of anatomy. Thirty figures are shown in various attitudes. Nearly all are nude, and as they scramble up the bank, buckling on their armor as they rush forward, eager for the fight, we see the wild, splendid swell of muscle and warm, tense, pulsing flesh. As an example of Michelangelo's consummate knowledge of form it was believed to be his finest work.

But it did not last long; the jealous Bandinelli made a strong bid for fame by destroying it. And thus do Bandinelli and Torrigiano go clattering down the corridors of time hand in hand. Yet we know what the picture was, for various men who saw it recorded their impressions; but although many of the younger artists of Italy flocked to Florence to see it, and many copied it, only one copy has come down to us—the one in the collection of the Earl of Leicester, at Holkham.

So even beautiful Florence could not treat her gifted son with impartiality, and when a call came from Pope Julius the Second, who had been elected in Fifteen Hundred Three, to return to Rome, the summons was promptly obeyed.

MICHELANGELO

ULIUS was one of the most active and vigorous rulers the earth has known. He had positive ideas on many subjects and like Napoleon "could do the thinking for a world." ✄ ✄

The first work he laid out for Michelangelo was a tomb, three stories high, with walls eighteen feet thick at the base, surrounded with numerous bas-reliefs and thirty heroic statues. It was to be a monument on the order of those worked out by the great Rameses, only incorporating the talent of Greece with that of ancient and modern Rome.

Michelangelo spent nearly a year at the Carrara quarries, getting out materials and making plans for forwarding the scheme. But gradually it came over him that the question of economy, which was deeply rooted in the mind of Julius, forbade the completion of such a gigantic and costly work. Had Julius given Michelangelo "carte-blanche" orders on the treasury, and not meddled with the plans, this surpassing piece of architecture might have found form. But the fiery Julius, aged seventy-four, was influenced by the architect Bramante to demand from Michelangelo a bill of expense and definite explanation as to details.

Very shortly after, Michelangelo quit work and sent a note to the Pope to the effect that the tomb was in the mountain of Carrara, with many beautiful statues, and if he wanted them he had better look for some one

MICHELANGELO

to get them out. As for himself, his address was Florence.
¶ The Pope sent couriers after him, one after another until five had been dispatched, but neither pleading, bribes nor threats could induce him to return.

As the scientist constructs the extinct animal from a thigh-bone, so we can guess the grandeur of what the tomb might have been from the single sample that has come down to us. The one piece of work that was completed for this tomb is the statue of "Moses." If the reputation of Michelangelo rested upon nothing else than this statue, it would be sufficient for undying fame. The "Moses" probably is better known than any other piece of Michelangelo's work. Copies of it exist in all important galleries; there are casts of it in fifty different museums in America, and pictures of it are numberless. There it stands in the otherwise obscure church of Saint Pietro in Vincolo today, one hand grasping the flowing beard, and the other sustaining the tables of the law—majesty, strength, wisdom beaming in every line. As Mr. Symonds has said, " It reveals the power of Pope Julius and Michelangelo fused into a Jove."

And so the messengers and messages were in vain, and even when the Pope sent an order to the Gonfaloniere Soderini, the actual ruler of Florence, to return the artist on pain of displeasure, the matter still rested— Michelangelo said he was neither culprit nor slave, and would live where he wished.

MICHELANGELO

At length the matter got so serious that it threatened the political peace of Florence, and in the goodly company of cardinals, bishops and chief citizens, Michelangelo was induced to go to Bologna and make peace with the Pope.

His first task now was a bronze statue of Julius, made, it is stated, as a partial reproduction of the "Moses." Descriptions of it declare it was even finer than the "Moses," but alas! it only endured four years, for a mob evolved it into a cannon to shoot stones, and at the same time ousted Julius from Bologna.

Michelangelo very naturally seconded the anathematization of the Bolognese by Julius, not so much for the insult to the Pope as for the wretched lack of taste they had shown in destroying a work of art. Had they left the beautiful statue there on its pedestal, Bologna would now on that account alone be a place of pilgrimage. The cannon they made is lost and forgotten—buried deep in the sand by its own weight—for Mein Herr Krupp can make cannon; but, woe betide us! who can make a statue such as Michelangelo made?

Michelangelo now followed the Pope to Rome and began a work that none other dare attempt, but which today excites the jealous admiration of every artist soul who views it—the ceiling of the Sistine Chapel. Ghirlandajo, Perugino, Botticelli and Luca Signorelli had worked on the walls with good effect, but to lie on one's back and paint overhead so as to bring out a

MICHELANGELO

masterly effect when viewed from seventy feet below was something they dare not attempt. Michelangelo put up his scaffolds, drew designs, and employed the best fresco artists in Italy to fill in the color. But as they used their brushes he saw that the designs became enfeebled under their attempts—they did not grasp the conception—and in wrath he discharged them all. He then obliterated all they had done, and shutting out the ceiling from every one but himself, worked alone. Often for days he would not leave the building, for fear some one would meddle with the work. He drew up food by a string and slept on the scaffold without changing his clothes.

After a year of intense application, no one but the artist had viewed the work. The Pope now demanded that he should be allowed to see it. A part of the scaffolding was struck, and the delight of the old Pope was unbounded. This was in Fifteen Hundred Nine, but the completed work was not shown to the public until All Souls' Day, Fifteen Hundred Twelve.

The guides at the Vatican tell us this ceiling was painted in twenty-two months, but the letters of Michelangelo, recently published, show that he worked on it over four years.

It contains over three hundred figures, all larger than life, and some are fifteen feet long. A complete description of the work Michelangelo did in this private chapel of the Pope would require a book, and in fact several

MICHELANGELO

books have been written with this ceiling as a subject. The technical obstacles to overcome in painting scenes and figures on an overhead surface can only be appreciated by those who have tried it. We can better appreciate the difficulties when we think that, in order even to view the decorations with satisfaction, large mirrors must be used, or one must lie prone on his back. In the ability to foreshorten and give harmonious perspective—supplying the effect of motion, distance, upright movement, coming toward you or moving away—all was worked out in this historic chapel in a way that has excited the wondering admiration of artists for three hundred years.

When the scaffolding was at last removed, the artist thought for a time he had done his last work. The unnatural positions he had been obliged to take had so strained the muscles of his neck that on the street he had often to look straight up at the sky to rest himself, and things on a straight line in front he could not distinguish. Eyes, muscles, hands, refused to act normally ⚜ ⚜

" My life is there on the ceiling of the Chapel of Sixtus," he said.

He was then thirty-nine years old.

Fifty eventful years of life and work were yet before him ⚜ ⚜

MICHELANGELO

HEN Pope Julius died, in Fifteen Hundred Thirteen, Leo the Tenth, a son of Lorenzo the Magnificent, was called to take his place. We might suppose that Leo would have remembered with pride the fact that it was his father who gave Michelangelo his first start in life, and have treated the great artist in the way Lorenzo would, were he then alive. But the retiring, abstemious habits of Michelangelo did not appeal to Leo. The handsome and gracious Raphael was his favorite, and at the expense of Michelangelo, Raphael was petted, feted and advanced. Hence arose that envious rivalry between these two great men, which reveals each in a light far from pleasant—just as if Rome were not big enough for both. The pontificate of Leo the Tenth lasted just ten years. On account of the lack of encouragement Michelangelo received, it seems the most fruitless season of his whole life ❧ ❧

Clement the Seventh, another member of the Medici family, succeeded Leo. Clement was too sensible of Michelangelo's merit to allow him to rust out his powers in petty tasks. He conceived the idea of erecting a chapel to be attached to the church of San Lorenzo, at Florence, to be the final resting-place of the great members of the Medici family. Michelangelo planned and built the chapel and for it wrought six great pieces of art. These are the statues of Lorenzo de Medici, father of Catherine de Medici (who was such a large,

MICHELANGELO

black blot on the page of history); a statue of Giuliano de Medici (whose name lives now principally because Michelangelo made this statue); and the four colossal reclining figures known as "Night," "Morning," "Dawn" and "Twilight." This chapel is now open to the public, and no visitor at Florence should miss seeing it ✄ ✄

The statue of Lorenzo must ever rank as one of the world's masterpieces. The Italians call it "Il Pensiero." The sullen strength of the attitude gives one a vague ominous impulse to get away. Some one has said that it fulfils Milton's conception of Satan brooding over his plans for the ruin of mankind.

In Fifteen Hundred Twenty-seven, while Michelangelo was working on the chapel, Florence was attacked and sacked by the Constable de Bourbon. The Medici family was again expelled, and from the leisurely decoration of a church in honor of the gentle Christ, the artist was called upon to build barricades to protect his native city. His ingenuity as an engineer was as consummate as his exquisite idea of harmony, and for nine months the city was defended.

Through treachery the enemy was then allowed to enter and Michelangelo fled. Riots and wars seem as natural as thunderstorms to the Latin people; but after a year the clouds rolled by, Michelangelo was pardoned, and went back to his work of beautifying the chapel of San Lorenzo ✄ ✄

MICHELANGELO

In Fifteen Hundred Thirty-four, Pope Clement was succeeded by Paul the Third. Paul was seventy years old, but the vigor of his mind was very much like that of the great Julius. His first desire was to complete the decoration of the Sistine Chapel, so that the entire interior should match the magnificence of the ceiling, and to the task he summoned Michelangelo.

The great artist hesitated. The ceiling was his supreme work as a painter, and he knew down deep in his heart that he could not hope to surpass it, and the risk of not equaling it was too great for him to run. The matter was too delicately personal to explain—only an artist could understand.

Michelangelo made excuses to the Pope and declared he had forgotten how to use a brush, that his eyesight was bad, and that the only thing he could do was to carve. But Paul was not to be turned aside, and reluctantly Michelangelo went back to the Sistine, that he had left over twenty years before.

Then it was that he painted " The Last Judgment " on the wall of the upper end of the chapel. Hamerton calls this the grandest picture ever executed, at the same time acknowledging its faults in taste. But it must be explained that the design was the conception of Julius, endorsed by Pope Paul, and it surely mirrors the spiritual qualities (or lack of them) in these men better than any biography possibly could.

The merciful Redeemer is shown as a muscular athlete,

MICHELANGELO

full of anger and the spirit of revenge—proud, haughty, fierce. The condemned are ranged before him—a confused mass of naked figures, suspended in all attitudes of agony and terrible foreboding. The " saved " are ranged on one side, and do not seem to be of much better intellectual and spiritual quality than the damned; very naturally they are quite pleased to think that it is the others who are damned, and not they. The entire conception reveals that masterly ability to portray the human figure in every attitude of fear or passion. A hundred years after the picture was painted, some dignitary took it into his head that portions of the work were too "daring"; and a painter was set at work robing the figures. His fussy attempts are quite apparent ⚹ Michelangelo's next work was to decorate the Paolina Chapel. As in his last work on the Sistine, he was constantly interrupted and advised and criticized. As he worked, cardinals, bishops and young artists watched and suggested, but still the " Conversion of Saint Paul " and the " Crucifixion of Saint Peter," in the Paolina, must ever rank as masterly art.

The frescoes in the Paolina Chapel occupied seven years and ended the great artist's career as a painter. He was seventy-three years old.

Pope Paul then made him Chief Architect of Saint Peter's. Michelangelo knew the difficulties to be encountered—the bickerings, jealousies and criticisms that were inseparable from the work—and was only

MICHELANGELO

moved to accept the place on Pope Paul's declaration that no one else could do as well, and that it was the will of God. Michelangelo looked upon the performance as a duty and accepted the task, refusing to take any recompense for his services. He continued to discharge the duties of the office under the direction of Popes Paul, Pius the Fourth and Pius the Fifth. In all he worked under the pontificates of seven different popes.

The dome of Saint Peter's, soaring to the skies, is his finest monument. The self-sustaining, airy quality in this stupendous structure hushes the beholder into silence; and yet that same quality of poise, strength and sufficiency marks all of the work of this colossus, whether it be painting, architecture or sculpture. America has paid tribute to Michelangelo's genius by reproducing the dome of Saint Peter's over the Capitol at Washington.

Michelangelo died at Rome, aged eighty-nine, working and planning to the last. His sturdy frame showed health in every part, and he ceased to breathe just as a clock runs down. His remains were secretly taken to Florence and buried in the church of Santa Croce. A fine bust marks the spot, but the visitor can not help feeling a regret that the dust of this marvelous man does not rest beneath the zenith of the dome of Saint Peter's at Rome.

MICHELANGELO

ITTING calmly in this quiet corner, and with closed eyes, viewing Michelangelo's life as a whole, the impression is one of heroic strength, battling with fierce passions, and becoming victor over them by working them up into art. The mold of the man was masculine, and the subdued sorrow that flavors his whole career never degenerates into sickly sentimentality or repining.

The sonnets of Michelangelo, recently given to the world, were written when he was nearly seventy years old. Several of the sonnets are directly addressed to Vittoria Colonna, and no doubt she inspired the whole volume. A writer of the time has mentioned his accidentally finding Michelangelo and Vittoria Colonna seated side by side in the dim twilight of a deserted church, " talking soft and low." Deserted churches have ever been favorite trysting-places for lovers; and one is glad for this little glimpse of quiet and peace in the tossing, troubled life-journey of this tireless man. In fact, the few years of warm friendship with Vittoria Colonna is a charmed and temperate space, without which the struggle and unrest would be so ceaseless as to be appalling. Sweet, gentle and helpful was their mutual friendship. At this period of Michelangelo's life we know that the vehemence of his emotions subsided, and tranquillity and peace were his for the rest of his life, such as he had never known before.

The woman who stepped out of high society and won

MICHELANGELO

the love of this stern yet gentle old man must have been of a mental and spiritual quality to command our highest praise. The world loves Vittoria Colonna because she loved Michelangelo, and led him away from strife and rivalry and toil.

REMBRANDT

REMBRANDT

The eyes and the mouth are the supremely significant features of the human face. In Rembrandt's portraits the eye is the center wherein life, in its infinity of aspect, is most manifest. Not only was his fidelity absolute, but there is a certain mysterious limpidity of gaze that reveals the soul of the sitter. A " Rembrandt " does not give up its beauties to the casual observer—it takes time to know it, but once known, it is yours forever.
—*Emile Michel*

REMBRANDT

SWIMMING uneasily in my ink-bottle is a small preachment concerning names, and the way they have been evolved, and lost, or added to. Some day I will fish this effusion out and give it to a waiting world. Those of us whose ancestors landed at Plymouth or Jamestown are very proud of our family names, and even if we trace quite easily to Castle Garden we do not always discard the patronymic.

Harmen Gerritsz was a young man who lived in the city of Leyden, Holland, in the latter part of the Sixteenth Century. The letters " sz " at the end of his name stood for " szoon " and signified that he was the szoon of Mynheer Gerrit.

Now Harmen Gerritsz duly served an apprenticeship with a miller, and when his time expired, being of an ambitious nature, he rented a mill on the city wall, and started business for himself. Shortly after he very naturally married the daughter of a baker.

All of Mr. Harmen Gerritsz's customers called him Harmen, and when they wished to be exact they spoke of him as Harmen van Ryn—that is to say, Harmen of the Rhine, for his mill was near the river. " Out West," even now, if you call a man Mister, he will probably

REMBRANDT

inquire what it is you have against him. ¶ Mr. and Mrs. Harmen lived in the mill, and as years went by were blessed with a nice little family of six children. The fifth child is the only one that especially interests us. They named him Rembrandt.

Rembrandt Harmenszoon van Ryn, he called himself when he entered at the grammar-school at Leyden, aged fourteen. His father's first name being Harmen, he simply took that, and discarded the Gerrit entirely, according to the custom of the time. In fact, all our Johnsons are the sons of John, and the names Peterson, Thompson and Wilson, in feudal times, had their due and proper significance. Then when we find names with a final ending of " s," such as Robbins, Larkins and Perkins, we are to understand that the owner is the son of his father. And so we find Rembrandt Harmenszoon in his later years writing his name Harmensz and then simply Harmens.

Mynheer Harmen Gerritszoon's windmill ground exceeding small, and the product found a ready market. There were no servants in the miller's family—everybody worked at the business. In Holland people are industrious. The leisurely ways of the Dutch can, I think, safely be ascribed to their environment, and here is an argument Buckle might have inserted in his great book, but did not, and so I will write it down.

There are windmills in Holland (I trust the fact need not longer be concealed) and these windmills are used

REMBRANDT

for every possible mechanical purpose. Now the wind blows only a part of the time—except in Chicago—and there may be whole days when not a windmill turns in all Holland. The men go out in the morning and take due note of the wind, and if there is an absolute calm many of them go back to bed. I have known the wind to die down during the day and the whole force of a windmill troop off to a picnic, as a matter of course. So the elements in Holland set man the example—he will not rush himself to death when not even the wind does.
¶ Then another thing: Holland has many canals. Farmers load their hay on canal-boats and take it to the barn, women go to market in boats, lovers sail, seemingly, right across the fields—canals everywhere ⚜ Traveling by canal is not rapid transit. So the people of Holland have plenty of precedent for moving at a moderate speed. There are no mountains in Holland, so water never runs; it may move, but the law of gravitation there only acts to keep things quiet. The Dutch never run footraces—neither do they scorch.
In Amsterdam I have seen a man sit still for an hour, and this with a glass of beer before him, gazing off into space, not once winking, not even thinking. You can not do that in America, where trolley-cars whiz and blizzards blow—there is no precedent for it in things animate or inanimate. In the United States everything is on the jump, art included.
Rembrandt Harmens worked in his father's mill, but

REMBRANDT

never strained his back. He was healthy, needlessly healthy, and was as smart as his brothers and sisters, but no smarter, and no better looking. He was exceedingly self-contained, and would sit and dream at his desk in the grammar-school, looking out straight in front of him—just at nothing.

The master tried flogging, and the next day found a picture of himself on the blackboard, his face portrayed as anything but lovely. Young Rembrandt was sent home to fetch his father. The father came.

"Look at that!" said the irate teacher; "see what your son did; look at that!"

Mynheer Harmen sat down and looked at the picture in his deliberate Dutch way, and after about fifteen minutes said, "Well, it does look like you!"

Then he explained to the schoolmaster that the lad was sent to school because he would not do much around the mill but draw pictures in the dust, and it was hoped that the schoolmaster could teach him something ✄ ✄

The schoolmaster decided that it was a hopeless case, and the miller went home to report to the boy's mother.

¶ Now, whenever a Dutchman is confronted by a problem too big to solve, or a task too unpleasant for him to undertake, he shows his good sense by turning it over to his wife. "You are his mother, anyway," said Harmen van Ryn, reproachfully.

The mother simply waived the taunt and asked, "Do

REMBRANDT

you tell me the schoolmaster says he will not do anything but draw pictures?"

"Not a tap will he do but make pictures—he can not multiply two by one."

"Well," said the mother, "if he will not do anything but draw pictures, I think we'd better let him draw pictures." ✖ ✖

REMBRANDT

T that early age I do not think Rembrandt was ambitious to be a painter. Good healthy boys of fourteen are not hampered and harassed by ambition—ambition, like love, camps hot upon our trail later. Ambition is the concomitant of rivalry, and sex is its chief promoter—it is a secondary sex manifestation.

The boy simply had a little intuitive skill in drawing, and the exercise of the talent was a gratification. It pleased him to see the semblance of face or form unfold before him. It was a kind of play, a working off of surplus energy.

Had the lad's mind at that time been forcibly diverted to books or business, it is very probable that today the catalogs would be without the name of Rembrandt ✳ But mothers have ambitions, even if boys have not— they wish to see their children do things that other women's children can not do. Among wild animals the mother kills, when she can, all offspring but her own. Darwin refers to mother-love as, " that instinct in the mind of the female which causes her to exaggerate the importance of her offspring—often protecting them to the death." Through this instinct of protection is the species preserved. In human beings mother-love is well flavored with pride, prejudice, jealousy and ambition. This is because the mother is a woman. And this is well —God made it all, and did He not look upon His work and pronounce it good?

REMBRANDT

The mother of Rembrandt knew that in Leyden there were men who painted beautiful pictures. She had seen these pictures at the University, and in the Town Hall and in the churches; and she had overheard men discussing and criticizing the work. She herself was poor and uneducated, her husband was only a miller, with no recreation beyond the beer-garden and a clicking reluctantly off to church in his wooden shoes on Sunday. They had no influential friends, no learned patrons—the men at the University never so much as nodded to millers. Her lot was lowly, mean, obscure, and filled with drudgery and pettiness. And now some one was saying her boy Rembrandt was lazy; he would neither work nor study. The taunt stung her mother-pride—
" He will do nothing but make pictures! "
Ah! a great throb came to her heart. Her face flushed, she saw it all—all in prophetic vision stood out like an etching on the blankness of the future. " He will do nothing but draw pictures? Very well then, he shall draw pictures! He will draw so well that they shall adorn the churches of Leyden, and the Town Hall, and yes! even the churches of Amsterdam. Holland shall be proud of my boy! He will teach other men to draw, his pictures will command fabulous prices, and his name shall be honored everywhere! Yes, my boy shall draw pictures! This day will I take him to Mynheer Jacob van Swanenburch, who was a pupil of the great Rubens, and who has scholars even from Antwerpen. I will take

REMBRANDT

him to the Master, and I will say: 'Mynheer, I am only a poor woman, the daughter of an honest baker. My husband is a miller. This is my son. He will do nothing but draw pictures. Here is a bag of gold—not much, but it is all good gold; there are no bad coins in this bag; I 've been ten years in saving them. Take this bag—it is yours—now teach my son to paint. Teach him as you taught Valderschoon and those others—my memory is bad, I can not remember the names—I 'm only a poor woman. Show my boy how to paint. And when I am dead, and you are dead, men will come to your grave and say, " It is here that he rests, here—the man who first taught Rembrandt Harmenszoon to use a brush!" Do you hear, Mynheer Van Swanenburch? The gold—it is yours—and this is my boy!'"

REMBRANDT

HE Van Swanenburches were one of the most aristocratic families of Leyden. Jacob van Swanenburch's father had been burgomaster, and he himself occupied from time to time offices of importance. He was not a great painter, although several specimens of his work still adorn the Town Hall of his native city.

Rembrandt was not very anxious to attend Swanenburch's classes. He was a hesitating, awkward youth, and on this account was regarded as unsocial. For a year the boy looked on, listened, and made straight marks and curves and all that. He did not read, and the world of art was a thing unknown to him.

There are two kinds of people to be found in all studios: those who talk about art, and the fellows who paint the pictures ✄ ✄

However, Rembrandt was an exception, and for a time would do neither. He would not paint, because he said he could not—anyway he would not; but no doubt he did a deal of thinking. This habit of reticence kept him in the background, and even the master had suspicions that he was too beefy to hold a clear mental conception ✄ The error of the Swanenburch atelier lay in the fact that quiet folks are not necessarily stupid. It is doubtless true, however, that stupid men by remaining quiet may often pass for men of wisdom: this is because no man can really talk as wisely as he can look ✄ ✄

REMBRANDT

Young Rembrandt was handicapped by a full-moon face, and small gray eyes that gave no glint, and his hair was so tousled and unruly that he could not wear a hat ⚜ ⚜
So the sons of aristocrats who cracked sly jokes at the miller's boy had their fun.
Rembrandt usually came in late, after the master had begun his little morning lecture. The lad was barefoot, having left his wooden shoon in the hallway " so as not to wear out the floor." He would bow awkwardly to the professor, fall over a chair or two that had been slyly pushed in his way, and taking his seat chew the butt end of a brush.
" Why are you always late? " asked the master one day ⚜ ⚜
" Oh, I was working at home and forgot the time." ⚜
" And what are you working at? "
" Me? I'm—I'm drawing a little," and he colored vermilion to the back of his neck.
" Well, bring your work here so we can profit by it," exclaimed a joker, and the class guffawed.
The next morning the lad brought his picture—a woman's face—a picture of a face, homely, wrinkled, weather-beaten, but with a look of love and patience and loyalty beaming out of the quiet eyes.
" Who did this? " demanded the teacher.
Rembrandt hesitated, stuttered, stammered, and then confessed that he did it himself—he could not tell a lie.

REMBRANDT

¶ He was sure the picture would be criticized and ridiculed, but he had decided to face it out. It was a picture of his mother, and he had sketched her just as she looked. He would let them laugh, and then at noon he would wait outside the door and smash the boy who laughed loudest over the head with a wooden shoe—and let it go at that.

But the scholars did not laugh, for Jacob van Swanenburch took the boy by the hand and leading him out before the class told those young men to look upon their master.

From that time forth Rembrandt was regarded by the little art world of Leyden as a prodigy.

Like William Cullen Bryant, who wrote "Thanatopsis" when scarcely eighteen, and writing for sixty years thereafter never equaled it, or Dante Gabriel Rossetti, who wrote "The Blessed Damozel" at the same age, Rembrandt sprang into life full-armed.

It is probably true that he could not then have produced an elaborate composition, but his faces were Rembrandtesque from the very first.

Rembrandt is the king of light and shade. You never mistake his work. As the years passed, around him clustered a goodly company of pupils, hundreds in all, who diligently worked to catch the trick, but Rembrandt stands alone. "He is the only artist who could ever paint a wrinkle," says Ruskin. All his portraits have the warts on. And the thought has often come to

REMBRANDT

me that only a Rembrandt—the only Rembrandt—could have portrayed the face of Lincoln. Plain, homely, awkward, eyes not mates, sunken cheeks, leathery skin, moles, uncombed hair, neckcloth askew; but over and above and beyond all a look of power—and the soul! that look of haunting sorrow and the great, gentle, compassionate soul within! ¶ And so there is a picture of Rembrandt's mother which this son painted that must ever stand out as one of the world's masterpieces. Let who will, declare that the portrait by Richter in the Gallery at Cologne, of Queen Louise, is the handsomest portrait ever painted; yet the depth of feeling, the dignity and love in the homely old mother's face, pale not in comparison, but are things to which the proud and beautiful Queen herself paid homage.

Rembrandt painted nearly a hundred pictures of his mother that we can trace. In most of them she holds in her hands a little Bible, and thus did the son pay tribute to her devoted piety. She was a model of which he never tired. He painted her in court dress, and various other fantastic garbs, that she surely never wore. He painted her as a nun, as a queen, a court beauty, a plain peasant, a musician; and in various large pictures her face and form are introduced. And most of these pictures of his mother are plainly signed with his monogram. He also painted his sister as the Madonna, and this is signed; but although he doubtless painted his father's face, yet he did not sign such

REMBRANDT

pictures, so their authenticity is a hazard. This fact gives a clue to his affections which each can work out for himself.

Rembrandt remained with Swanenburch for three years, and the master proved his faithful friend. He gave him an introduction into the aristocratic art world which otherwise might have barred its doors against so profound a genius, as aristocracy has done time and again.
¶ The best artists are not necessarily the best teachers. If a man has too much skill along a certain line he will overpower and kill the individuality in his pupil. There are teachers who smother a pupil with their own personality, and thus it often happens that the strongest men are not the most useful as instructors. The ideal teacher is not the one who bends all minds to match his own; but the one who is able to bring out and develop the good that is in the pupil—him we will crown with laurel ≫ ≫

Swanenburch was pretty nearly the ideal teacher. His good nature, the feminine quality of sympathy in his character, his freedom from all petty, quibbling prejudice, and his sublime patience all worked to burst the tough husk, and develop that shy and sensitive, yet uncouth and silent youth, bringing out the best that was in him. A wrong environment in those early years might easily have shaped Rembrandt into a morose and resentful dullard: the good in his nature, thrown back upon itself, would have been turned to gall.

REMBRANDT

HE little business on the city wall had prospered, and Harmen van Ryn moved, with his family, out of the old mill into a goodly residence across the street. He was carrying his head higher, and the fact that his son Rembrandt was being invited to the homes of the professors at the University was incidentally thrown off, until the patrons at the beer-garden grew aweary and rapped their glasses on the table as a signal for silence.

Swanenburch had given a public exhibition of the work of his pupils, at which young Rembrandt had been pushed forward as an example of what right methods in pedagogics could do.

" Well, why can not all your scholars draw like that, then? " asked a broad-beamed Dutchman.

" They certainly could, if they would follow the principles I lay down," answered the master severely ⚓ But admiration did not spoil Rembrandt. His temperature was too low for ebullition—he took it all quite as a matter of course. His work was done with such ease that he was not aware it was extraordinary in quality; and when Swanenburch sold several of his sketches at goodly prices and put the silver in the lad's hand, he asked who the blockheads were who had invested.

Swanenburch taught his pupils the miracle of spreading a thin coat of wax on a brass plate, and drawing a picture in the wax with a sharp graver; then acid was poured over it and the acid ate into the brass so as to

REMBRANDT

make a plate from which you could print. Etching was a delight to Rembrandt. Expert illustrators of books were in demand at Leyden, for it was then the bookmaking center of Northern Europe. The Elzevirs were pushing the Plantins of Antwerp hard for first place.

So skilfully did Rembrandt sketch, that one of the great printers made a proposition to his father to take the boy until he was twenty-one, and pay the father a thousand florins a year for the lad's services as an illustrator. The father accepted the proposition; and the next day brought around another Harmenszoon, who he declared was just as good. But the bookmaker was stubborn and insisted on having a certain one or none. So the bargain fell through.

It was getting near four years since Swanenburch had taken Rembrandt into his keeping, and now he went to the boy's parents and said: " I have given all I have to offer to your son. He can do all I can, and more. There is only one man who can benefit him and that is Pieter Lastman, of Amsterdam. He must go and study with the great Lastman—I myself will take him."

Lastman had spent four years in Italy, and had come back full to overflowing with classic ideas. His family was one of the most aristocratic in Amsterdam, and whatever he said concerning art was quoted as final. He was the court of last appeal. His rooms were filled with classic fragments, and on his public days visitors flocked to hear what he might have to say about the wonders of

REMBRANDT

Venice, Florence and Rome. For in those days men seldom traveled out of their own countries, and those who did had strange tales to tell the eager listeners when they returned.

Lastman was handsome, dashing, popular. His pictures were in demand, principally because they were Lastman's. Proud ladies came from afar and begged the privilege of sitting as his model. In Italy, Lastman had found that many painters employed 'prentice talent. The great man would sketch out the pictures, and the boys would fill in the color. Lastman would go off about his business, and perhaps drop in occasionally during the day to see how the boys got on, adding a few touches here and there, and gently rebuking those who showed too much genius. Lastman believed in genius, of course; but only his own genius filled his ideal. As a consequence all of Lastman's pictures are alike—they are all equally bad. They represent neither the Italian school nor the Dutch, being hybrids: Italian skies and Holland backgrounds; Dutchmen dressed as dagoes.

Lastman was putting money in his purse. He closely studied public tastes, and conformed thereto. He was popular, and there is in America today a countryman of his, of like temperament, who is making much moneys out of literature by similar methods.

Into Lastman's keeping came the young man, Rembrandt Harmens. Lastman received him cordially, and set him to work.

REMBRANDT

But the boy proved hard to manage: he had his own ideas about how portraits should be painted. ¶ Lastman tried to unlearn him. The master was patient, and endeavored hard to make the young man paint as he should—that is, as Lastman did; but the result was not a success. The Lastman intellect felt sure that Rembrandt had no talent worth encouraging.

Lastman produced a great number of pictures, and his name can be found in the catalogs of the galleries of Amsterdam, Munich, Berlin and Antwerp; and his canvases are in many of the old castles and palaces of Germany. In recent years they have been enjoying a vogue, simply because it was possible that Rembrandt had worked on them. All the "Lastmans" have been gotten out and thoroughly dusted by the connoisseurs, in a frantic search for earmarks.

The perfect willingness of Lastman to paint a picture on any desired subject, and have it ready Saturday night, all in the colors the patron desired, with a guarantee that it would give satisfaction, filled the heart of Rembrandt with loathing.

At the end of six months, when he signified a wish to leave, it was a glad relief to the master. Lastman had tried to correct Rembrandt's vagaries as to chiaroscuro, but without success. So he wrote an ambiguous letter certifying to the pupil's "having all his future before him," gave him a present of ten florins in jingling silver, and sent him back to his folks

REMBRANDT

EMBRANDT had been disillusioned by his stay in the fashionable art-world of Amsterdam. Some of his idols had crumbled, and there came into his spirit a goodly dash of pessimism. His father was disappointed and suggested that he get a place as illustrator at the bookmakers, before some one else stepped in and got the job.

But Rembrandt was not ambitious. He decided he would not give up painting, at least not yet—he would keep at it and he would paint as he pleased. He had lost faith in teachers. He moped around the town, and made the acquaintance of the painter Engelbrechtsz and his talented pupil, Lucas van Leyden. Their work impressed him greatly, and he studied out every detail on the canvases until he had absorbed the very spirit of the artist. Then, when he painted, he very naturally took their designs, and treated them in his own way. Indeed, the paucity in invention of those early days must ever impress the student of art.

In visiting the galleries of Europe, I made it my business to secure a photograph of every " Madonna and Babe " of note that I could find. My collection now numbers over one hundred copies, with no two alike.

The Madonna, of course, is the extreme example; but there are dozens of " The Last Supper," " Abraham's Sacrifice," " The Final Judgment," " The Brazen Serpent," " Raising of Lazarus," " The Annunciation," " Rebekah at the Well " and so on.

REMBRANDT

If one painter produced a notable picture, all the other artists in the vicinity felt it their duty to treat the same subject; in fact, their honor was at stake—they just had to, in order to satisfy the clamor of their friends, and meet the challenges of detractors.

This " progressive sketching " was kept up, each man improving, or trying to improve, on the attempts of the former, until a Leonardo struck twelve and painted his " Last Supper," or a Rubens did his " Descent From the Cross "—then competitors grew pale, and tried their talent on a lesser theme.

One of the most curious examples of the tendency to follow a bellwether is found in the various pictures called " The Anatomy Lesson." When Venice was at its height, in the year Fourteen Hundred Ninety-two—a date we can easily remember—an unknown individual drew a picture of a professor of anatomy; on a table in the center is a naked human corpse, while all around are ranged the great doctor's pupils. Dissection had just been introduced into Venice at that time, and in a treatise on the subject by Andrea Vesali, I find that it became quite the fad. The lecture-rooms were open to the public, and places were set apart for women visitors and the nobility, while all around the back were benches for the plain people. On the walls were skeletons, and in cases were arranged saws, scalpels, needles, sponges and various other implements connected with the cheerful art.

REMBRANDT

The Unknown's picture of this scene made a sensation. And straightway other painters tried their hands at it, the unclothed form of the corpse affording a fine opportunity for the " classic touch." Paul Veronese tried it, and so did the Bellinis—Titian also.

Then a century passed, as centuries do, and the glory of Venice drifted to Amsterdam—commercially and artistically. Amsterdam painters used every design that the Venetians had, and some of their efforts were sorry attempts. In Sixteen Hundred Twenty, following Venetian precedent, dissection became a fad in Leyden and Amsterdam. Swanenburch engraved a picture of the Leyden dissecting-room, with a brace of gallant doctors showing some fair ladies the beauties of the place. The Dutch were ambitious—the young men, Rembrandt included, drew pictures entitled, " The Lesson in Anatomy." Doctors who were getting on in the world gave orders for portraits, showing themselves as about to begin work on a subject. One physician, with intent to get even with his rival, had the artist picture the rival in the background as a pupil. Then the rival ordered a picture of himself, proud and beautiful, giving a lesson in anatomy, armed and equipped for business, and the cadaver was—the other doctor.

At the Chicago Fair, in Eighteen Hundred Ninety-three, there was shown a most striking " Anatomy Lesson " from the brush of a young New York artist. It pictures the professor removing the sheet from the

REMBRANDT

face of the corpse, and we behold the features of a beautiful young woman.

Some day I intend to write a book entitled, "The Evolution and Possibilities of the Anatomy Lesson." Keep your eye on the subject—we are not yet through with it.

¶ Swanenburch offered to give Rembrandt a room in his own house, but he preferred the old mill, and a wheat-bin was fitted up for a private studio. The fittings of the studio must have cost fully two dollars, according to all accounts; there were a three-legged stool, an easel, a wooden chest, and a straw bed in the corner. Only one window admitted the light, and this was so high up that the occupant was not troubled by visitors looking in.

Our best discoveries are the result of accident.

This single window, eight feet from the ground, allowed the rays of light to enter in a stream. On cloudy days and early in the mornings or in the evenings, Rembrandt noted that when the light fell on the face of the visitor the rest of the body was wholly lost in the shadow. He placed a curtain over the window with a varying aperture cut in it, and with his mother as model made numerous experiments in the effects of light and shade. He seems to have been the very first artist who could draw a part of the form, leaving all the rest in absolute blackness, and yet give the impression to the casual onlooker that he sees the figure complete. Plain people with no interest in the technique of art will look upon

REMBRANDT

a "Rembrandt," and go away and describe things in the picture that are not there. They will declare to you that they saw them—those obvious things which one fills in at once with his inward eye. For instance, there is a portrait of a soldier, by Rembrandt, in the Louvre, and above the soldier's head you see a tall cockade. You assume at once that this cockade is in the soldier's hat, but no hat is shown—not the semblance nor the outline of a hat. There is a slight line that might be the rim of a hat, or it might not. But not one person out of a thousand, looking upon the picture, but would go away and describe the hat, and be affronted if you should tell them there is no hat in the picture. Given a cockade, we assume a hat.

By the use of shadows Rembrandt threw the faces into relief; he showed the things he wished to show and emphasized one thing by leaving all else out. The success of art depends upon what you omit from your canvas. This masterly effect of illusion made the son of the miller stand out in the Leyden art-world like one of his own etchings.

Curiously enough, the effect of a new model made Rembrandt lose his cunning; with strangers he was self-conscious and ill at ease. His mother was his most patient model; his father and sisters took their turn; and then there was another model who stood Rembrandt in good stead. And that was himself. We have all seen children stand before a mirror and make

REMBRANDT

faces. Rembrandt very early contracted this habit, and it evidently clung to him through life. He has painted his own portrait with expressions of hate, fear, pride, mirth, indifference, hope and wrath shown on his plastic features ✣ ✣

There is also an old man with full white beard and white hair that Rembrandt has pictured again and again ✣ This old man poses for "Lot," "Abraham," "Moses," "A Beggar," "A King," and once he even figures as "The Almighty." Who he was we do not know, and surely he did not realize the honor done him, or he would have written a proud word of explanation to be carved on his tomb.

REMBRANDT

N the Stuttgart Museum is a picture entitled, "Saint Paul in Prison," signed by Rembrandt, with the date Sixteen Hundred Twenty-seven. "The Money-Changers" in the Berlin Gallery bears the same signature and date. Rembrandt was then twenty years of age, and we see that he was doing good work. We also know that there was a certain market for his wares.

When twenty-two years of age his marvelous effects of light and shade attracted people who were anxious to learn how to do it. According to report he had sixteen pupils in Sixteen Hundred Twenty-eight, each of whom paid him the fixed sum of one hundred florins. This was not much, but it gave him an income equal to that of his father, and tended to confirm his faith in his own powers.

¶ His energy was a surprise to all who had known him, for besides teaching his classes he painted, sketched and etched. Most of his etchings were of his own face—not intended as portraits, for they are often purposely disguised. It seemed to be the intent of the artist to run the whole gamut of the passions, portraying them on the human face. Six different etchings done in the year Sixteen Hundred Twenty-eight are to be seen in the British Museum.

His most intimate friend at this time was Jan Lievens. The bond that united them was a mutual contempt for Lastman of Amsterdam. In fact, they organized a club, the single qualification required of each candidate for

REMBRANDT

admittance being a hatred for Lastman. This club met weekly at a beer-hall, and each member had to relate an incident derogatory to the Lastman school. At the close of each story, all solemnly drank eternal perdition to Lastman and his ilk. Finally, Lastman was invited to join; and in reply he wrote a gracious letter of acceptance. This surely shows that Lastman was pretty good quality, after all.

Rembrandt was making money. His pupils spread his praise, and so many new ones came that he took the old quarters of Swanenburch.

In Sixteen Hundred Thirty-one, there came to him a young man who was to build a deathless name for himself—Gerard Dou. Then to complete the circle came Joris van Vliet, whose reputation as an engraver must ever take a first rank. Van Vliet engraved many of Rembrandt's pictures, and did it so faithfully and with such loving care that copies today command fabulous prices among the collectors. Indeed, we owe to Van Vliet a debt for preserving many of Rembrandt's pictures, the originals of which have disappeared. With the help of Van Vliet the Elzevirs accomplished their wishes, and so made use of the talent of Rembrandt ❧

Rembrandt lived among the poor, as a matter of artistic policy, mingling with them on an absolute equality. He considered their attitudes simpler, more natural, and their conduct less artificial, than the manners of those in higher walks.

REMBRANDT

About Sixteen Hundred Twenty-nine, there came into his hands a set of Callot's engravings, and the work produced on his mind a profound impression. Callot's specialty was beggardom. He pictured decrepit beggars, young beggars, handsome girl-beggars, and gallant old beggars who wore their fluttering rags with easy grace. ¶ The man who could give the phlegmatic Rembrandt a list to starboard must have carried considerable ballast. Straightway on making Callot's acquaintance he went forth with bags of coppers and made the acquaintance of beggars. He did not have to travel far— " the Greeks were at his door." The news spread, and each morning, the truthful Orles has told us, " there were over four hundred beggars blocking the street that led to his study," all willing to enlist in the cause of art. For six months Rembrandt painted little beside " the ragged gentry." But he gradually settled down on about ten separate and distinct types of abject picturesqueness ✄ ✄

Ten years later, when he pictured the " Healing Christ," he introduced the Leyden beggars, and these fixed types that he carried hidden in the cells of his brain he introduced again and again in various pictures. In this respect he was like all good illustrators: he had his properties, and by new combinations made new pictures. Who has not noticed that every painter carries in his kit his own distinct types—sealed, certified to, and copyrighted by popular favor as his own personal

REMBRANDT

property? ¶ Can you mistake Kemble's "coons," Denslow's dandies, Remington's horses, Giannini's Indians, or Gibson's "Summer Girl"? These men may not be Rembrandts, but when we view the zigzag course art has taken, who dare prophesy that this man's name is writ in water and that man's carved in the granite of a mountain-side! Contemporary judgments usually have been wrong. Did the chief citizens of Leyden in the year Sixteen Hundred Thirty regard Rembrandt's beggars as immortal? Not exactly!

REMBRANDT

N Sixteen Hundred Thirty-one, Rembrandt concluded that his reputation in the art-world of Holland was sufficient for him to go to Amsterdam and boldly pit himself against De Keyser, Hals, Lastman and the rest. He had put forth his "Lesson in Anatomy," and the critics and connoisseurs who had come from the metropolis to see it were lavish in their praise. Later we find him painting the subject again with another doctor handling the tweezers and scalpel.

Rembrandt started for Amsterdam the second time—this time as a teacher, not as a scholar. He rented an old warehouse on the canal for a studio. It was nearly as outlandish a place as his former quarters in the mill at Leyden. But it gave him plenty of room, was secluded, and afforded good opportunity for experiments in light and shade.

He seemed to have gotten over his nervousness in working with strange models; for new faces now begin to appear. One of these is that of a woman, and it would have been well for his art had he never met her. We see her face quite often, and in the "Diana Bathing" we behold her altogether.

Rembrandt shows small trace of the classic instinct, for classic art is founded on poetic imagination. Rembrandt painted what he saw; the Greeks portrayed that which they felt; and when Rembrandt paints a Dutch wench and calls her "Diana," he unconsciously illustrates the

REMBRANDT

difference between the naked and the nude. Rembrandt painted this same woman, wearing no clothes to speak of, lolling on a couch; and evidently considering the subject a little risky, thought to give it dignity by a Biblical title: "Potiphar's Wife." One good look at this picture, and the precipitate flight of Joseph is fully understood. We feel like following his example.

Rembrandt had simply haunted the dissecting-rooms of the University at Leyden a little too long.

The study of these viragos scales down our rating of the master. Still, I suppose every artist has to go through this period—the period when he thinks he is called upon to portray the feminine form divine—it is like the mumps and the measles.

After a year of groping for he knew not what, with money gone, and not much progress made, Rembrandt took a reef in his pride and settled down to paint portraits, and to do a little good honest teaching.

Scholars came to him, and commissions for portraits began to arrive. He renounced the freaks of costume, illumination and attitude, and painted the customer in plain, simple Dutch dress. He let "Diana" go, and went soberly to work to make his fortune.

Holland was prosperous. Her ships sailed every sea, and brought rich treasures home. The prosperous can afford to be generous. Philanthropy became the fad. Charity was in the air, and hospitals, orphanages and homes for the aged were established. The rich merchants felt it an honor to serve on the board of managers of these institutions.

In each of the guildhalls were parlors set apart for deliberative gatherings; and it became the fashion to embellish these rooms with portraits of the managers, trustees and donors.

Rembrandt's portraits were finding their way to the guilds. They attracted much attention, and orders came —orders for more work than the artist could do. He doubled his prices in the hope of discouraging applicants.

¶ Studio gossip and society chatter seemed to pall on young Rembrandt. It is said that when a 'bus-driver has a holiday he always goes and rides with the man who is taking his place; but when Rembrandt had a holiday he went away from the studio, not towards it. He would walk alone, off across the meadows, and along the canals, and once we find him tramping thirty miles to visit cousins who were fishermen on the seacoast. Happy fisher-folk!

But Rembrandt took few play-spells; he broke off entirely from his tavern companions and lived the life of an ascetic and recluse, seeing no society except the society that came to his studio. His heart was in his art, and he was intent on working while it was called the day ☙ ☙

About this time there came to him Cornelis Sylvius, the eminent preacher, to sit for a picture that was to adorn the Seaman's Orphanage, of which Sylvius was director.

REMBRANDT

It took a good many sittings to bring out a Rembrandt portrait. On one of his visits the clergyman was accompanied by a young woman—his ward—by name, Saskia van Ulenburgh.
The girl was bright, animated and intelligent, and as she sat in the corner the painter sort of divided his attention between her and the clergyman. Then the girl got up, walked about a bit, looking at the studio properties, and finally stood behind the young painter, watching him work. This was one of the things Rembrandt could never, never endure. It paralyzed his hand, and threw all his ideas into a jumble. It was the law of his studio that no one should watch him paint— he had secrets of technique that had cost him great labor ✄ ✄
"You do not mind my watching you work?" asked the ingenuous girl.
"Oh, not in the least!"
"You are quite sure my presence will not make you nervous, then?"
Rembrandt said something to the effect that he rather liked to have some one watch him when he worked; it depended, of course, on who it was—and asked the sitter to elevate his chin a little and not look so cross ✄
Next day Saskia came again to watch the transfer of the good uncle's features to canvas.
The young artist was first among the portrait-painters of Amsterdam, and had a long waiting-list on his

71

REMBRANDT

calendar, but we find he managed to paint a portrait of Saskia about that time. We have the picture now and we also have four or five other pictures of her that Rembrandt produced that year. He painted her as a queen, as a court lady and as a flower-girl. The features may be disguised a little, but it is the same fine, bright, charming, petite young woman.

Before six months had passed he painted several more portraits of Saskia; and in one of these she has a sprig of rosemary—the emblem of betrothal—held against her heart.

And then we find an entry at the Register's to the effect that they were married on June Twenty-fourth, Sixteen Hundred Thirty-four.

Rembrandt's was a masterly nature: strong, original and unyielding. But the young woman had no wish that was not his, and her one desire was to make her lover happy. She was not a great woman, but she was good, which is better, and she filled her husband's heart to the brim. Those first few years of their married life read like a fairy-tale.

He bought her jewels, laces, elegant costumes, and began to fill their charming home with many rare objects of art. All was for Saskia—his life, his fortune, his work, his all.

As the years go by we shall see that it would have been better had he saved his money and builded against the coming of the storm; but even though Saskia protested

REMBRANDT

mildly against his extravagance, the master would have his way ❧ ❧

His was a tireless nature: he found his rest in change. He usually had some large compositions on hand and turned to this for pastime when portraits failed. Then Saskia was ever present, and if there was a holiday he painted her as the "Jewish Bride," "The Gypsy Queen," or in some other fantastic garb.

We have seen that in those early years at Leyden he painted himself, but now it was only Saskia—she was his other self. All those numerous pictures of himself were drawn before he knew Saskia—or after she had gone ❧ ❧

Their paradise continued nine years—and then Saskia died ❧ ❧

Rembrandt was not yet forty when desolation settled down upon him.

REMBRANDT

ASKIA was the mother of five children; four of them had died, and the babe she left, Titus by name, was only eight months old when she passed away.

For six months we find that Rembrandt did very little. He was stunned, and his brain and hand refused to co-operate ✥ ✥

The first commission he undertook was the portrait of the wife of one of the rich merchants of the city. When the work was done, the picture resembled the dead Saskia so much more than it did the sitter that the patron refused to accept it. The artist saw only Saskia and continued to portray her.

But work gave him rest, and he began a series of Biblical studies—serious, sober scenes fitted to his mood. His hand had not lost its cunning, for there is a sureness and individuality shown in his work during the next few years that stamps him as the Master.

But his rivals raised a great clamor against his style. They declared that he trampled on all precedent and scorned the laws on which true art is built. However, he had friends, and they, to help him, went forth and secured the commission—the famous "Night-Watch," now in the Ryks Museum at Amsterdam.

The production of this fine picture resulted in a comedy of errors, that shaded off into a tragedy for poor Rembrandt. The original commission for this picture came from thirty-seven prominent citizens, who were

REMBRANDT

to share the expense equally among them. The order was for the portraits of the eminent men to appear on one canvas, the subjects to be grouped in an artistic way according to the artist's own conceit.

Rembrandt studied hard over the matter, as he was not content to execute a picture of a mass of men doing nothing but pose.

It took a year to complete the picture. The canvas shows a band of armed men, marching forth to the defense of the city in response to a sudden night alarm. Two brave men lead the throng and the others shade off into mere Rembrandt shadows, and you only know there are men there by the nodding plumes, banners and spearheads that glisten in the pale light of the torches.

When the picture was unveiled, the rich donors looked for themselves on the canvas, and some looked in vain. Only two men were satisfied, and these were the two who marched in the vanguard.

"Where am I?" demanded a wealthy shipowner of Rembrandt as the canvas was scanned in a vain search for his proud features.

"You see the palace there in the picture, do you not?" asked the artist petulantly.

"Yes, I see that," was the answer.

"Well, you are behind that palace."

The company turned on Rembrandt, and forbade the hanging of any more of his pictures in the municipal buildings ✼ ✼

REMBRANDT

Rembrandt shrugged his shoulders. But as the year passed and orders dropped away, he found how unwise a thing it is to affront the public. Men who owed him refused to pay, and those whom he owed demanded their money.

He continued doggedly on his course.

Some years before he had bought a large house and borrowed money to pay for it, and had further given his note at hand to various merchants and dealers in curios. As long as he was making money no one cared for more than the interest, but now the principal was demanded. So sure had Rembrandt been of his powers that he did not conceive that his income could drop from thirty thousand florins a year to scarcely a fifth of that.

Then his relations with Hendrickje Stoffels had displeased society. She was his housekeeper, servant and model—a woman without education or refinement, we are told. But she was loyal, more than loyal, to Rembrandt: she lived but to serve him and sought to protect his interests in every way. When summoned before the elders of the church to answer for her conduct, she appeared, pleaded guilty and shocked the company by declaring, " I would rather go to Hell with Rembrandt Harmens than play a harp in Heaven, surrounded by such as you! "

The remark was bruited throughout the city and did Rembrandt no good. His rivals combined to shut his work out of all exhibitions, and several made it their

REMBRANDT

business to buy up the overdue claims against him.
¶ Then officers came and took possession of his house, and his splendid collections of jewels, laces, furniture, curios and pictures were sold at auction. The fine dresses that once belonged to Saskia were seized: they even took her wedding-gown: and wanton women bid against the nobility for the possession of these things. Rembrandt was stripped of his sketches, and these were sold in bundles—the very sweat of his brain for years. Then he was turned into the streets.

But Hendrickje Stoffels still clung to him, his only friend. Rembrandt's proud heart was broken. He found companionship at the taverns; and to get a needful loaf of bread for Hendrickje and his boy, made sketches and hawked them from house to house.

Fashions change and art is often only a whim. People wondered why they had ever bought those dark, shadowy things made by that Leyden artist, What's-his-name! One man utilized the frames which contained "Rembrandts" by putting other canvases right over in front of them.

Rembrandt's son Titus tried his skill at art, but with indifferent success. He died while yet a youth. Then Hendrickje passed away, and Rembrandt was alone—a battered derelict on the sea of life. He lost his identity under an assumed name, and sketched with chalk on tavern-walls and pavement for the amusement of the crowd ❧ ❧

REMBRANDT

He died in Sixteen Hundred Sixty-nine, and the expense of his burial was paid by the hands of charity.
The cost of the funeral was seven dollars and fifty cents.
¶ In Eighteen Hundred Ninety-seven, there was sold in London a small portrait by Rembrandt for a sum equal to a trifle more than thirty-one thousand dollars. But even this does not represent the true value of one of his pictures—for connoisseurs regard a painting by Rembrandt as priceless.
There is a law in Holland forbidding any one on serious penalty to remove a "Rembrandt" from the country. If any one of the men who combined to work his ruin is mentioned in history, it is only to say, "He lived in the age of Rembrandt."

RUBENS

RUBENS

I was admitted to the Duke of Lerma's presence, and took part in the embassy. The Duke exhibited great satisfaction at the excellence and number of the pictures, which surely have acquired a certain fair appearance of antiquity (by means of my retouching), in spite even of the damage they had undergone. They are held and accepted by the King and Queen as originals, without there being any doubt on their side, or assertion on ours, to make them believe them to be such.
—*Letter From Rubens at Madrid, to Chieppo, Secretary of the Duke of Mantua*

RUBENS

HE father of Peter Paul Rubens was a lawyer, a man of varied attainments and marked personality. In statecraft he showed much skill, and by his ability in business management served William the Silent, Prince of Orange, in good stead ⚜ ⚜

But Jan Rubens had a bad habit of thinking for himself. The habit grew upon him until the whisper was passed from this one to that, that he was becoming decidedly atheistic ⚜ ⚜

Spain held a strong hand upon Antwerp, and the policy of Philip the Second was to crush opposition in the bud. Jan Rubens had criticized Spanish rule, and given it as his opinion that the Latin race would not always push its domination upon the people of the North.

At this time Spain was so strong that she deemed herself omnipotent, and was looking with lustful eyes towards England. Drake and Frobisher and Walter Raleigh were learning their lessons in seafaring; Elizabeth was Queen; while up at Warwickshire a barefoot boy named William Shakespeare was playing in the meadows, and romping in the lanes and alleys of Stratford ⚜ ⚜

All this was taking place at the time when Jan Rubens

RUBENS

was doing a little thinking on his own account. On reading the history of Europe, Flanders seems to one to have been a battle-ground from the dawn of history up to the night of June Eighteenth, Eighteen Hundred Fifteen, with a few incidental skirmishes since, for it is difficult to stop short. And it surely was meet that Napoleon should have gone up there to receive his Waterloo, and charge his cavalry into a sunken roadway, making a bridge across with a mingled mass of men and horses; upon which site now is a huge mound thrown up by the English, surmounted by a gigantic bronze lion cast from the captured cannon of the French ☙ ☙

Napoleon belonged to the Latin race: he pushed his rule north into Flanders, and there his prowess ended—there at the same place where Spanish rule had been throttled and turned back upon itself. "Thus far, and no farther." Jan Rubens was right. But he paid dearly for his prophecy.

When William the Silent was away on his many warfaring expeditions, the man who had charge of certain of his affairs was Jan Rubens. Naturally this brought Rubens into an acquaintanceship with the wife of the silent prince. Rubens was a handsome man, ready in speech, and of the kind that makes friends easily. And if the wife of the Prince of Orange liked the vivacious Rubens better than the silent warrior (who won his sobriquet, they do say, through density of emotion and

RUBENS

lack of ideas), why, who can blame her! ¶ But Rubens had a wife of his own, to whom he was fondly attached; and this wife was also the close and trusted friend of the woman whose husband was off to the wars. And yet when this dense and silent man came back from one of his expeditions, it was only publicly to affront and disgrace his wife, and to cast Jan Rubens into a dungeon. No doubt the Prince was jealous of the courtly Rubens—and the Iagos are a numerous tribe. But Othello's limit had been reached. He damned the innocent woman to the lowest pit, and visited his wrath on the man ✄ ✄

Of course I know full well that all Northern Europe once rang with shrill gossip over the affair, and as usual the woman was declared the guilty party. Even yet, when topics for scandal in Belgium run short, this old tale is revived and gone over—sides being taken. I've gone over it, too, and although I may be in the minority, just as I possibly am as to the " guilt " of Eve, yet I stand firm on the side of the woman. I give the facts just as they appear, having canvassed the whole subject, possibly a little more than was good for me.

Republics may be ungrateful, but the favor of princes is fickle as the East Wind.

We make a fine hullabaloo nowadays because France or Russia occasionally tries and sentences a man without giving him an opportunity of defense; but in the Sixteenth Century the donjon-keeps of hundreds of

RUBENS

castles in Europe were filled with prisoners whose offense consisted in being feared or disliked by some whimsical local ruler.

Jan Rubens was sent on an official errand to Dillenburg, and arriving there was seized and thrown into prison, without trial or the privilege of communicating with his friends.

Months of agonizing search on the part of his wife failed to find him, and the Prince only broke the silence long enough to usurp a woman's privilege by telling a lie, and declaring he did not know where Rubens was, "but I believe he has committed suicide through remorse." ⚜ ⚜

The distracted wife made her way alone from prison to prison, and finally, by bribing an official, found her husband was in an underground cell in the fortress at Dillenburg. It was a year before she was allowed to communicate with or see him. But Maria Rubens was a true diplomat. You move a man not by going to him direct, but by finding out who it is that has a rope tied to his foot. She secured the help of the discarded wife of the Prince, and these two managed to interest a worthy bishop, who brought his influence to bear on Count John of Nassau. This man had jurisdiction of the district in which the fortress where Rubens was confined was located; and he agreed to release the prisoner on parole on condition that a deposit of six thousand thalers be left with him, and an agreement signed

RUBENS

by the prisoner that he would give himself up when requested; and also, further, that he would acknowledge before witnesses that he was guilty of the charges made against him.

The latter clause was to justify the Prince of Orange in his actions toward him.

Rubens refused to plead guilty, even for the sake of sweet liberty, on account of the smirch to the name of the Princess.

But on the earnest request of both his wife and the "co-respondent," he finally accepted the terms in the same manner that Galileo declared the earth stood still. Rubens got his liberty, was loyal to his parole, but John of Nassau kept the six thousand thalers for "expenses."

So much for the honor of princes; but in passing it is worthy of recall that Jan Rubens pleaded guilty of disloyalty to his wife, on request of said wife, in order that he might enjoy the society of said wife—and cast a cloud on the good name of another woman on said woman's request.

So here is a plot for a play: a tale of self-sacrifice and loyalty on the part of two women that puts to shame much small talk we hear from small men concerning the fickleness and selfishness of woman's love. "Brief as woman's love!" said Hamlet—but then, Hamlet was crazy.

Jan Rubens died in Cologne, March Eighteenth, Fifteen

RUBENS

Hundred Eighty-seven, and lies buried in the Church of Saint Peter. Above the grave is a slab containing this inscription: "Sacred to the Memory of Jan Rubens, of Antwerp, who went into voluntary exile and retired with his family to Cologne, where he abode for nineteen years with his wife Maria, who was the mother of his seven children. With this his only wife Maria he lived happily for twenty-six years without any quarrel. This monument is erected by said Maria Pypelings Rubens to her sweetest and well-deserved husband."

Of course, no one knew then that one of the seven—the youngest son of Jan and Maria—was to win deathless fame, or that might have been carved on the slab, too, even if something else had to be omitted.

But Maria need not have added that last clause, stating who it was that placed the tablet: as it stands we should all have known that it was she who dictated the inscription. Epitaphs are proverbially untruthful; hence arose the saying, " He lies like an epitaph." The woman who can not evolve a good lie in defense of the man she loves is unworthy of the name of wife.

The lie is the weapon of defense that kind Providence provides for the protection of the oppressed. " Women are great liars," said Mahomet; " Allah in his wisdom made them so."

Hail, Maria Rubens! turned to dust these three hundred years, what star do you now inhabit? or does your avatar live somewhere here in this world? At the

RUBENS

thought of your unselfish loyalty and precious fibbing, an army of valiant, ghostly knights will arise from their graves, and rusty swords leap from their scabbards if aught but good be said against thee.

"Ho, ho! and was n't your husband really guilty, and did n't you know it all the time?" I 'll fling my glove full in the face of any man who dare ask you such a question ✄ ✄

Beloved and loving wife for six-and-twenty years, and mother of seven, looking the world squarely in the eye and telling a large and beautiful untruth, carving it in marble to protect your husband's name, I kiss my hand to you!

RUBENS

N the doorpost of a queer little stone house in Cologne is carved an inscription to the effect that Peter Paul Rubens was born there on June Twenty-ninth, Fifteen Hundred Seventy-seven. It is probably true that the parents of Rubens lived there, but Peter Paul was born at Siegen, under the shadow of a prison from which his father was paroled.

After a few years the discipline relaxed, for there were new prisoners coming along, and Maria and Jan were given permission to move to Cologne.

Peter Paul was ten years of age when his father died. The next year the widow moved with her little brood back to Antwerp, back to the city from which her husband had been exiled just twenty years before. Five years previous the Prince of Orange, who had exiled her husband, was himself sent on a journey, via the dagger of an assassin. As the chief enemy of Jan Rubens was dead, it was the hope of the widow to recover their property that had been confiscated.

Maria Rubens was a good Catholic; and she succeeded in making the authorities believe that her husband had been, too, for the home that Royalty had confiscated was returned to her.

The mother of Peter Paul loved the dim twilight mysteries of the Church, and accepted every dogma and edict as the literal word of God. It is easier and certainly safer to leave such matters to the specialists.

RUBENS

She was a born diplomat. She recognized the power of the Church and knew that to win one must go with the current, not against it. To have doubts, when the Church is willing to bear the whole burden, she thought very foolish. Had she been a man she would have been a leader among the Jesuits. The folly of opposition had been shown her most vividly in her husband's career. What could he not have been had he been wise and patient and ta'en the tide at its flood! And this was the spirit that she inculcated in the minds of her children.
¶ Little Peter Paul was a handsome lad—handsome as his father—with big, dark brown eyes and clustering curls. He was bright, intelligent, and blessed with a cheerful, obliging disposition. He came into the world a welcome child, carrying the beauty of the morning in his face, and form, and spirit.
No wonder is it that the Countess de Lalaing desired the boy for a page as soon as she saw him. His mother embraced the opportunity to let her favorite child see court life, and so at the early age of twelve, at a plunge, he began that career in polite diplomacy that was to continue for half a century.
The Countess called herself his " other mother," and lavished upon him all the attention that a childless woman had to bestow. The mornings were sacred to his lessons, which were looked after by a Jesuit priest; and in the afternoon, another priest came to give the ladies lessons in the languages, and at these circles young

RUBENS

Peter Paul was always present as one of the class. ¶ Indeed, the earliest accomplishment of Peter Paul was his polyglot ability. When he arrived at Antwerp, a mere child, he spoke German, Flemish and French.

Such a favorite did little Peter Paul become with his "other mother," and her ladies of the court, that his sure-enough mother grew a bit jealous, and feared they would make a hothouse plant of her boy, and so she took him away.

The question was, for what profession should he be educated? That he should serve the Church and State was already a settled fact in the mother's mind: to get on in the world you must cultivate and wisely serve those who are in power—that is, those who have power to bestow. Priests were plentiful as blackberries, and politicians were on every corner, and many of the priests and officeseekers had no special talent to recommend them. They were simply timeservers. Maria knew this: To get on you must have several talents, otherwise people will tire of you.

In Cologne, Maria Rubens had met returned pilgrims from Rome and they had told her of that trinity of giants, Michelangelo, Raphael and Leonardo; and how these men had been the peers of prince and pope, because they had the ability to execute marvelous works of beauty.

This extraordinary talent called attention to themselves, so they were summoned out of the crowd and became

RUBENS

the companions and friends of the greatest names of their time. ¶ And then, how better can one glorify his Maker than by covering the sacred walls of temples with rich ornament!

The boy entered into the project, and the mother's ambition that he should retrieve his father's fortune fired his heart. Thus does the failure in life of a parent often give incentive to the genius of a son.

Tobias Verhaecht was the man who taught Rubens the elements of drawing, and inculcated in him that love of Nature which was to be his lifelong heritage. The word "landscape" is Flemish, and it was the Dutch who carried the term and the art into England. Verhaecht was among the very first of landscape-painters. He was a specialist: he could draw trees and clouds, and a winding river, but could not portray faces. And so he used to call in a worthy portrait-painter, by the name of Franck, to assist him whenever he had a canvas on the easel that demanded the human form. Then when Franck wanted background and perspective, Verhaecht would go over with a brush and a few pots of paint and help him out.

At fifteen, the keen, intuitive mind of Rubens had fathomed the talents of those two worthies, Verhaecht and Franck. His mind was essentially feminine: he absorbed ideas in the mass. Soon he prided himself on being able to paint alone as good a picture as the two collaborators could together. Yet he was too wise to

RUBENS

affront them by the boast. The bent of his talent he thought was toward historical painting; and more than this, he knew that only epic art would open the churches for a painter. And so he next became a pupil under Adam van Noort. This man was a rugged old character, who worked out things in his own way and pushed the standard of painting full ten points to the front. His work shows a marked advance over that of his contemporaries and over the race of painters that preceded him. Every great artist is the lingering representative of an age that is dead, or else he is the prophet and forerunner of a golden age to come.

When I visited the Church of Saint Jaques in Antwerp, where Rubens lies buried, the good old priest who acted as guide called my attention to a picture by Van Noort, showing Peter finding the money in the mouth of the fish. "A close study of that picture will reveal to you the germ of the Rubens touch," said the priest, and he was surely right: its boldness of drawing, the strong, bright colors and the dexterity in handling all say, "Rubens." Rubens builded on the work of Van Noort.

¶ Twenty years after Rubens had left the studio of Van Noort he paid tribute to his old master by saying, "Had Van Noort visited Italy and caught the spirit of the classicists, his name would stand first among Flemish artists."

Rubens worked four years with Van Noort and then entered the studio of Otto van Veen. This man was not

RUBENS

a better painter than Van Noort, but he occupied a much higher social position, and Peter Paul was intent on advancing his skirmish-line. He never lost ground. Van Veen was Court Painter, and on friendly terms with the Archduke Albert, and Isabella, his wife, daughter of Philip the Second, King of Spain.

Van Veen took very few pupils—only those who had the ability to aid him in completing his designs. To have worked with this master was an introduction at once into the charmed circle of royalty.

Rubens was in no haste to branch out on his own account: he was quite content to know that he was gaining ground, making head upon the whole. He won the confidence of Van Veen at once by his skill, his cheerful presence, and ability to further the interests of his master and patrons. In Fifteen Hundred Ninety-nine, when Rubens was twenty-two, he was enrolled as a free master at the Guild of Saint Luke on the nomination of Van Veen, who also about this time introduced the young artist to Albert and Isabella.

But the best service that Van Veen did for Rubens was in taking him into his home and giving him free access to the finest collection of Italian art in the Netherlands. These things filled the heart of Rubens with a desire to visit Italy, and there to dive deeply into the art spirit of that land from which all our art has sprung.

To go abroad then and gain access to the art treasures of the world was not a mere matter of asking for a

RUBENS

passport, handing out a visiting-card, and paying your way ◎ ◎

Young men who wished to go abroad to study were required to pass a stiff examination. If it was believed that they could not represent their own country with honor, their passports were withheld. And to travel without a passport was to run the risk of being arrested as an absconder.

But Rubens' place in society was already secure. Instead of applying for his passports personally and undergoing the usual catechization, his desires were explained to Van Veen, and all technicalities were waived, as they always are when you strike the right man. Not only were the passports forthcoming, but Albert and Isabella wrote a personal note to Viccuzo Gonzaga, the Duke of Mantua, commending the young painter to the Duke's good offices.

Van Veen further explained to Rubens that to know the Duke of Mantua might mean either humiliation or crowning success. To attain the latter through the Duke of Mantua, it was necessary to make a good impression on Annibale Chieppo, the Duke's Minister of State. Chieppo had the keeping of the ducal conscience as well as the key to the strong-box.

The Duke of Mantua was one of those strange loaded dice that Fate occasionally flings upon this checkerboard of time: one of those characters whose feverish faculties border on madness, yet who do the world

RUBENS

great good by breaking up its balances, preventing social ankylosis, and eventually forcing upon mankind a new deal. But in the train of these vagrant stars famine and pestilence follow.

The Duke of Mantua was brother in spirit to the man who made Versailles—and making Versailles undid France.
¶ Versailles is a dream: no language that the most enthusiastic lovers of the beautiful may utter, can exaggerate the wonders of those acres of palaces and miles of gardens. The magnificence of the place makes the ready writer put up his pencil, and go away whipped, subdued and crestfallen to think that here are creations that no one pen can even catalog. Louis the Grand, we are told, had thirty-six thousand men and six thousand horses at work here at one time. No wonder Madame De Maintenon was oppressed by the treasures that were beyond the capacity of man to contemplate; and so off in the woods was built that lover's retreat, "The Trianon." And out there today, hidden in the forest, we behold the second Trianon, built by Marie Antoinette, and we also see those straw-thatched huts where the ladies of her Court played at peasant life.

Louis the Fourteenth builded so well that he discouraged his successor from doing anything but play keephouse, and so extensively that France was rent in twain, and so mightily that even Napoleon Bonaparte was staggered at the thought of maintaining Versailles.
¶ " It's too much for any man to enjoy—I give it up!"

RUBENS

said the Little Man, perplexed, and ordered every door locked and every window tightly shuttered. Then he placed a thousand men to guard the place and went about his business.

But today Versailles belongs to the people of France; more, it belongs to the people of earth: all is free and you may carry away all the beauty of the place that your soul can absorb.

Now, who shall say that Louis the Fourteenth has not enriched the world?

The Duke of Mantua was sumptuous in his tastes, liberal, chivalrous, voluptuous, extravagant. At the same time he had a cultivated mind, an eye for proportion, and an ear for harmony. He was even pious at times, and like all debauchees had periods of asceticism. He was much given to gallantry, and his pension-list of beautiful women was not small. He was a poet and wrote some very good sonnets; he was a composer who sang, from his own compositions, after the wine had gone round; he was an orator who committed to memory and made his own the speeches that his secretary wrote ❧ ❧

He traveled much, and in great state, with a retinue of servants, armed guards, outriders and guides. Wherever he went he summoned the local poet, or painter, or musician, and made a speech to him, showing that he was familiar with his work by humming a tune or quoting a stanza. Then he put a chain of gold around

RUBENS

the poor embarrassed fellow's neck, and a purse in his hands, and the people cheered.

When he visited a town, cavalcades met him afar out, and as he approached, little girls in white and boys dressed in velvet ran before and strewed flowers in front of his carriage.

Oh, the Duke of Mantua was a great man!

In his retinue was a troop of comedians, a court fool, two dwarfs for luck, seven cooks, three alchemists and an astrologer. Like the old woman who lived in a shoe, he had so many children he did n't know what to do. One of his sons married a princess of the House of Saxony, another son was a cardinal, and a daughter married into the House of Lorraine. He had alliances and close relations with every reigning family of Europe. The sister of his wife, Marie de Medici, became " King of France," as Talleyrand avers, and had a mad, glad, sad, bad, jolly time of it.

Wherever the Duke of Mantua went, there too went Annibale Chieppo, the Minister of State. This man had a calm eye, a quiet pulse, and could locate any man or woman in his numerous retinue at any hour of the day or night. He was a diplomat, a soldier, a financier.

You could not reach the Duke until you had got past Chieppo ❧ ❧

And the Duke of Mantua had much commonsense— for in spite of envy and calumny and threat he never lost faith in Annibale Chieppo.

RUBENS

No success in life is possible without a capable first mate. Chieppo was king of first mates.
He was subtle as Richelieu and as wise as Wolsey.
When Peter Paul Rubens, aged twenty-three, arrived at Venice, the Duke of Mantua and his train were there. Rubens presented his credentials to Chieppo, and the Minister of State read them, looked upon the handsome person of the young man, proved for himself he had decided talent as a painter, put him through a civil-service examination—and took him into favor. Such a young man as this, so bright, so courtly, so talented, must be secured. He would give the entire Court a new thrill.
"Tomorrow," said the Minister of State, "tomorrow you shall be received by the Duke of Mantua and his court!"

RUBENS

THE ducal party remained at Venice for several weeks, and when it returned to Mantua, Rubens went along quite as a matter of course. From letters that he wrote to his brother Philip, as well as from many other sources, we know that the art collection belonging to the Duke of Mantua was very rich. It included works by the Bellinis, Correggio, Leonardo da Vinci, Andrea del Sarto, Tintoretto, Titian, Paoli Veronese, and various others whose names have faded away like their colors.

Rubens had long been accustomed to the ways of polite society. The magnificence of his manner, and the fine egotism he showed in his work, captivated the Court. The Duke was proud of his ward and paraded him before his artistic friends as the coming man, incidentally explaining that it was the Duke of Mantua who had made him and not he himself.

It was then the custom of those who owned masterpieces to have copies made and present them to various other lovers of the beautiful. If an honored guest was looking through your gallery, and expressed great pleasure in a certain canvas, the correct thing was to say, " I'll have my best painter make a copy of it, and send it to you "—and a memorandum was made on an ivory tablet. This gracious custom seems to have come down from the time when the owners of precious books constantly employed scribes and expert illuminators

RUBENS

in making copies for distribution. The work done in the scriptoriums of the monasteries, we know, was sent away as presents, or in exchange for other volumes.

Rubens set diligently to work copying in the galleries of Mantua; and whether the Duke was happier because he had discovered Rubens than Rubens was because he had found the Duke, we do not know. Anyway, all that the young painter had hoped and prayed for had been sent him.

Here was work from the very hands of the masters he had long worshiped from afar. His ambition was high and his strong animal spirits and tireless energy were a surprise to the easy-going Italians. The galleries were his without let or hindrance, save that he allow the ladies of the Court to come every afternoon and watch him work. This probably did not disturb him; but we find the experienced Duke giving the young Fleming some good advice, thus: "You must admire all these ladies in equal portion. Should you show favoritism for one, the rest will turn upon you; and to marry any one of them would be fatal to your art."

Rubens wrote the advice home to his mother, and the good mother viseed it and sent it back.

After six months of diligent work at Mantua we find Rubens starting for Rome with letters from the Duke to Cardinal Montalto, highly recommending him to the good graces of the Cardinal, and requesting, " that you will be graciously so good as to allow our Fleming

RUBENS

to execute and make copies for us of such paintings as he may deem worthy."

Cardinal Montalto was a nephew of Pope Sixtus, and the strongest man, save the Pope, in Rome. He had immense wealth, great learning, and rare good sense in matters of art. He was a close friend of the Duke of Mantua; and to come into personal relations with such a man was a piece of rare good fortune for any man. The art world of Rome now belonged to Rubens—all doors opened at his touch. "Our Fleming" knew the value of his privileges. "If I do not succeed," he writes to his mother, "it will be because I have not improved my opportunities." The word fail was not in his lexicon. His industry never relaxed. In Walpole's "Anecdotes of Painting," an account is given of a sketchbook compiled by Rubens at this time. The original was in the possession of Maurice Johnson, of Spalding, England, in Eighteen Hundred Forty-five, at which time it was exhibited in London and attracted much attention.

I have seen a copy of the book with its hundred or more sketches of the very figures that we now see and admire in the Uffizi and Pitti galleries and in the Vatican. Eight generations of men have come and gone since Rubens sketched from the Old Masters, but there today stand the chiseled shapes, which were then centuries old, and there today are the "Titians" and the "Raphaellos" just as the exuberant Fleming saw them. Surely this must show us how short are the days

RUBENS

of man! "Open then the door; you know how little while we have to stay!"

The two figures that seemed to impress Rubens most, as shown in the sketchbook, are the Farnese "Hercules" and Michelangelo's "David." He shows the foot of the "Hercules," and the hand of the "David," and gives front, back and side views with comments and criticisms. Then after a few pages have been covered by other matter he goes back again to the "Hercules"—the subject fascinates him.

When we view "The Crucifixion," in the Cathedral at Antwerp, we conclude that he admired the "Hercules" not wisely but too well, for the muscles stand out on all the figures, even of the Savior, in pure Farnese style. Two years after that picture was painted, he did his masterpiece, "The Descent From the Cross," and we behold with relief the change that had come over the spirit of his dreams. Mere pride in performing a difficult feat had given place to a higher motive. There is no reason to suppose that the Apostles had trained to perform the twelve labors of Hercules, or that the two Marys were Amazons. But the burly Roman forms went back to Flanders, and for many years staid citizens were slipped into classic attitudes to do duty as Disciples, Elders, Angels—all with swelling biceps, knotted muscles, and necks like the Emperor Vespasian.

¶ The Mantuan Envoy at Rome had private orders from Chieppo to see that the Fleming was well treated.

RUBENS

The Envoy was further requested to report to the Secretary how the painter spent his time, and also how he was regarded by Cardinal Montalto. Thus we see the wily Secretary set one servant watching another, and kept in close touch with all.

The reports, however, all confirmed the Secretary in his belief that the Fleming was a genius, and, moreover, worthy of all the encouragement that was bestowed upon him. The Secretary sent funds from time to time to the painter, with gentle hints that he should pay due attention to his behavior, and also to his raiment, for the apparel oft doth proclaim the man.

The Duke of Mantua seems to have regarded Rubens as his own private property, and Rubens had too much sense to do anything by word or deed that might displease his patron.

When he had gotten all that Italy could give, or more properly all he could absorb, his intent was to follow his heart and go straight back to Flanders.

Three years had passed since Rubens had arrived in Venice—years of profit to both spirit and purse. He had painted pictures that placed him in the rank of acknowledged artists, and the Duke of Mantua had dropped all patronizing airs. With the ducal party Rubens had visited Verona, Florence, Pisa and Padua. His fame was more than local. The painter hinted to Chieppo that he would like to return to Antwerp, but the Secretary objected—he had important work for him.

RUBENS

UBENS was from Flanders, and Flanders was a Spanish possession: then the Fleming knew the daughter of the King of Spain. No man was so well fitted to go on a delicate diplomatic mission to Spain as the Flemish painter. " You are my heart's jewel," said the Duke of Mantua to the Prime Minister, when the Minister suggested it.
¶ The Duke wished private information as to certain things Spanish, and was also preparing the way to ask for sundry favors. The Court at Madrid was artistic in instinct; so was the Mantuan Court. To recognize the esthetic side of your friend's nature, when your friend is secretly not quite sure but that he is more worldly than spiritual, is a stroke of diplomacy. Spain was not really artistic, but there were stirrings being felt, and Velasquez and Murillo were soon to appear.

The Duke of Mantua wished to present the King of Spain with certain pictures; his mind was filled with a lively sense of anticipation of future favors to be received—which feeling we are told is gratitude. The entire ceremony must be carried out appropriately—the poetic unities being fully preserved. Therefore a skilful painter must be sent with the pictures, in order to see that they were safely transported, properly unpacked, and rightly hung.

Instructions were given to Peter Paul Rubens, the artistic ambassador, at great length, as to how he should proceed. He was to make himself agreeable to

RUBENS

the King, and to one greater than the King—the man behind the throne—the Duke of Lerma; and to several fair ladies as well.

The pictures were copies of the masters—"Titians," "Raphaellos," "Tintorettos" and "Leonardos." They were copied with great fidelity, even to the signature and private marks of the original artist. In fact, so well was the work done that if the recipient inclined to accept them as originals, his mind must not be disabused. Further, the envoy was not supposed to know whether they were originals or not (even though he had painted them), and if worse came to worst he must say, "Well, surely they are just as good as the originals, if not better."

Presents were taken for a dozen or more persons. Those who were not so very artistic were to have gifts of guns, swords and precious stones. The ambassador was to travel in a new carriage, drawn by six horses and followed by wagons carrying the art treasures. All this so as to make the right impression and prove to Madrid that Mantua was both rich and generous. And as a capsheaf to it all, the painter must choose an opportune moment and present his beautiful carriage and horses to the King, for the belief was rife that the King of Spain was really more horsey than artistic.

The pictures were selected with great care, and the finest horses to be found were secured, regardless of cost. Several weeks were consumed in preparations, and

RUBENS

at last the cavalcade started away, with Rubens in the carriage and eleven velvet suits in his chest, as he himself has told us. It was a long, hard journey to Madrid. There were encounters with rapacious landlords, and hairbreadth escapes in the imminent deadly customhouse. But in a month the chromatic diplomat arrived and entered Madrid at the head of his company, wearing one of the velvet suits, and riding a milk-white charger ❧ ❧

Rubens followed orders and wrote Signor Chieppo at great length, giving a minute account of every incident and detail of the journey and of his reception at Madrid. While at the Court he kept a daily record of happenings, which was also forwarded to the Secretary.

These many letters have recently been given to the public. They are in Italian, with a sprinkling here and there of good honest Dutch. All is most sincere, grave and explicit. Rubens deserved great credit for all these letters, for surely they were written with sweat and lamp-smoke. The work of the toiler is over all, but we must remember that at that time he had been studying Italian only about a year.

The literary style of Rubens was Johnsonese all his life, and he made his meaning plain only by repetitions and many rhetorical flounderings. Like the average sixteen-year-old boy who sits himself down and takes his pen in hand, all his sprightliness of imagination vanished at sight of an ink-bottle. With a brush his feelings were

RUBENS

fluid, and in a company grace dwelt upon his lips; but when asked to write it out he gripped the pen as though it were a crowbar instead of a crow's-quill.

But Chieppo received his reports; and we know the embassy was a success—a great success. The debonair Fleming surprised the King by saying, "Your Majesty, it is like this"—and then with a few bold strokes drew a picture.

He modestly explained that he was not much of a painter —" merely used a brush for his own amusement "—and then made a portrait for the Minister of State that exaggerated all of that man's good points, and ignored all his failings. There was a cast in the Minister's eye, but Rubens waived it. The Minister was delighted, and so was the King. He then made a portrait of the King that was as flattering as portraits should be that are painted for monarchs.

Among his other accomplishments the Fleming was a skilful horseman; he rode with such grace and dash that the King took him on his drives, Rubens riding by the side of the carriage, gaily conversing as they rode.

And so with the aid of his many talents he won the confidence of the King and Court and was initiated into the inner life of Spanish royalty in a way that Iberta, the Mantuan Resident, never had been. The King liked Rubens, and so did the Man behind the Throne.

¶ Mortals do not merely like each other because they like each other; such a bond is tenuous as a spider's

RUBENS

thread. I love you because you love the things that I love. One woman won my heart by her subtle appreciation of "The Dipsy Chanty." Men meet on a horse basis, a book basis, a religious basis, or some other mutual leaning; sometimes we find them uniting on a mutual dislike for something. For instance, I have a friend to whom I am bound by the tie of oneness because we dislike olives, and have a mutual indifference to the pretended claims of the unpronounceable Pole who wrote "Quo Vadis." The discovery was accidentally made in a hotel dining-room: we clasped hands across the board, and since then have been as brothers ❧ ❧

The more points at which you touch humanity the more friends you have—the greater your influence. Rubens was an artist, a horseman, a musician, a politician and a gourmet. When conceptions in the kitchen were vague, he would send for the cook and explain to him how to do it. He possessed a most discriminating palate and a fine appreciation of things drinkable. These accomplishments secured him a well-defined case of gout while yet a young man. He taught the Spanish Court how to smoke, having himself been initiated by an Englishman, who was a companion of Sir Walter Raleigh, and showed them how to roll a cigarette while engaged in ardent conversation. And the Spaniards have not yet lost the art, for once in Cadiz I saw a horse running away, and the driver rolled and lighted a

RUBENS

cigarette before trying to stop the mad flight of the frantic brute.

In the Royal Gallery at Madrid are several large paintings by Rubens that were doubtless done at this time. They are religious subjects; but worked in, after the manner of a true diplomat, are various portraits of brave men and handsome women. To pose a worthy senator as Saint Paul, and a dashing lady of the Court as the Holy Virgin, was most gratifying to the phrenological development of approbativeness of the said senator and lady. Then, as the painter had pictured one, he must do as much for others, so there could be no accusation of favoritism.

Thus the months passed rapidly. The Duke of Lerma writes to Chieppo, " We desire your gracious permission to keep the Fleming another month, as very special portraits are required from his brush."

The extra month extended itself to three; and when at last Rubens started back for Mantua it was after a full year's absence.

The embassy was a most complete success. The diplomat well masked his true errand with the artist's garb: and who of all men was ever so well fitted by Nature to play the part as Rubens?

Yet he came near overdoing the part at least once. It was in this wise: he really was not sure that the honors paid him were on account of his being a painter or a courtier. But like comedians who think their forte is

RUBENS

tragedy, so the part of courtier was more pleasing to Rubens than that of painter, because it was more difficult. He painted with such ease that he set small store on the talent: it was only a makeshift for advancement.
¶ Don John, Duke of Braganza, afterward King of Portugal, was a lover of art, and desired to make the acquaintance of the painter. So he wrote to Rubens at Madrid, inviting him to Villa Vitiosa, his place of residence. ¶ Rubens knew how the Duke of Mantua did these things—he decided to follow suit.

With a numerous train, made up from the fringe of the Madrid Court, with hired horsemen going before, and many servants behind, the retinue started away. Coming within five miles of the villa of Don John, word was sent that Rubens and his retinue awaited his embassy. ¶ Now Don John was a sure-enough duke and could muster quite a retinue of his own on occasion, yet he had small taste for tinsel parades. Men who have a real good bank-balance do not have to wear fashionable clothes. Don John was a plain, blunt man who liked books and pictures. He wanted to see the painter, not a courtier: and when he heard of the style in which the artist was coming, he just put a boy on a donkey and sent word out that he was not at home. And further, to show the proud painter his place, he sent along a small purse of silver to pay the artist for the trouble to which he had been. The rebuke was so delicate that it was altogether lost on Rubens—he was simply enraged.

RUBENS

N all, Rubens spent eight years in the service of the Duke of Mantua. He had visited the chief cities of Italy, and was familiar with all the art of the golden ages that had gone before. When he left Italy he had to take advantage of the fact that the Duke was in France, for every time before, when he had suggested going, he was questioned thus: "Why, have you not all you wish? What more can be done for you? Name your desire and you shall have it."

But Rubens wanted home: Antwerp, his mother, brothers, sister, the broad River Scheldt, and the good old Flemish tongue.

Soon after arriving in Antwerp he was named as Court Painter by Albert and Isabella. Thus he was the successor of his old master, Van Veen.

He was now aged thirty-two, in possession of an income from the State, and a fame and name to be envied. He was rich in money, jewels and art treasures brought from Italy, for he had the thrifty instincts of a true Dutchman

And it was a gala day for all Antwerp when the bells rang and the great organ in the Cathedral played the wedding-march when Peter Paul Rubens and Isabella Brandt were married, on the Thirteenth of October, Sixteen Hundred Nine. Never was there a happier mating

That fine picture at Munich of Rubens and his wife tells

RUBENS

of the sweet comradeship that was to be theirs for many years. He opened a school, and pupils flocked to him from all Europe; commissions for work came and orders for altar-pieces from various churches.

An order was issued by the Archduke that he should not leave Holland, and a copy of the order was sent to the Duke of Mantua, to shut off his importunities.

Among the pupils of Rubens we find the name of Jordaens (whom he had first known in Italy), De Crayer, Anthony Van Dyck, Franz Snyder and many others who achieved distinction. Rubens was a positive leader; so animated was his manner that his ambition was infectious. All his young men painted just as he did. His will was theirs. From now on, out of the thousands of pictures signed " P. P. Rubens," we can not pick out a single picture and say, " Rubens did this." He drew outlines and added the finishing touches; and surely would not have signed a canvas of which he did not approve. In his great studio at Antwerp, at various times, fully a hundred men worked to produce the pictures we call " Rubens."

Those glowing canvases in the " Rubens Gallery " of the Louvre, showing the history and apotheosis of Marie de Medici, were painted at Antwerp. The joyous, exuberant touch of Rubens is over all, even though the work was done by 'prentice hands.

Peaceful lives make dull biographies, and in prosperity is small romance.

RUBENS

We may search long before finding a life so full to overflowing of material good things as that of Rubens. All he touched turned to gold. From the time he returned to Antwerp in Sixteen Hundred Eight to his death in Sixteen Hundred Forty, his life-journey was one grand triumphal march. His many diplomatic missions were simply repetitions of his first Spanish embassy, with the Don John incident left out, for Don John seems to have been the only man who was not at home to the gracious Rubens.

Mr. Ruskin has said: "Rubens was a great painter, but he lacked that last undefinable something which makes heart speak to heart. You admire, but you never adore. No real sorrow ever entered his life."

Perhaps we get a valuable clue in that last line. Great art is born of feeling, and the heart of Rubens was never touched by tragedy, nor the rocky fastnesses of his tears broken in upon by grief. In many ways his was the spirit of a child: he had troubles, but not sufficient to prevent refreshing sleep, and when he awoke in the morning the trials of yesterday were gone.

Even when the helpful, faithful and loving Isabella Brandt was taken away from him by death, there soon came other joys to take the place of those that were lost.
¶ We have full fifty pictures of his second wife: she looks down at us—smiling, buxom, content—from every gallery-wall in Europe. Rubens was fifty-three and she was sixteen when they were married; and were

RUBENS

it not for a twinge of gout now and then, he would have been as young as she.

When Rubens went to England on " an artistic commission," we see that he captured Charles the First just as he captured the court of Spain. He painted five portraits of the King that we can trace. The mild-mannered Charles was greatly pleased with the fine portrait of himself bestriding the prancing cream-colored charger.

Several notable artists, Sir Joshua Reynolds among them, have complimented the picture by taking the horse, background and pose, and placing another man in the saddle—or more properly, taking off the head of Charles the First and putting on the head of any bold patron who would furnish the price. In looking through the galleries of Europe, keep your eye out for equestrian portraits, and you will be surprised to see on your tab, when you have made the rounds, how many painters have borrowed that long-maned, yellow horse that still rears in the National Gallery in London, smelling the battle afar off—as Charles himself preferred to smell it.

¶ Rubens had a good time in England, although his patience was severely tried by being kept at painting for months, awaiting an opportune time to give King Charles some good advice on matters political.

English ways were very different from those of the Continent, but Rubens soon spoke the language with fluency, even if not with precision.

RUBENS

Rubens spoke seven languages, and to speak seven languages is to speak no one well. On this point we have a little comment from high authority. Said Charles the First, writing to Buckingham, "The Fleming painter prides himself on being able to pass for an Englishman, but his English is so larded with French, Dutch and Italian that we think he must have been employed on the Tower of Babel."

While painting the ceiling of the banqueting-room at Whitehall (where a Dutchman was later to be crowned King of England), he discussed politics with the Duke of Buckingham and the King, from the scaffold. Some years after we find Buckingham visiting Rubens at his home in Antwerp, dickering for his fine collection of curios and paintings.

The Duke afterwards bought the collection and paid Rubens ten thousand pounds in gold for it.

Every one complimented Rubens on his shrewdness in getting so much money for the wares, and Rubens gave a banquet to his friends in token of the great sale to the Britisher. It was a lot of money, to be sure, but the Englishman realized the worth of the collection better than did Rubens. We have a catalog of the collection. It includes nineteen Titians, thirteen Paul Veroneses, seventeen Tintorettos, three Leonardos, three Raphaels and thirteen pictures by Rubens himself.

A single one of the Titians, if sold at auction today, would bring more than the Duke paid for the entire

RUBENS

collection. ¶ James McNeil Whistler has said, " There may be a doubt about Rubens having been a Great Artist; but he surely was an Industrious Person." There is barely enough truth in Mr. Whistler's remark, taken with its dash of wit, to save it; but Philip Gilbert Hamerton's sober estimate is of more value: " The influence of Rubens for good can not be overestimated. He gave inspiration to all he met, and his example of industry, vivid imagination, good-cheer and good taste have had an incalculable influence on art. We have more canvases from his hand than from the hand of any other master. And these pictures are a quarry to which every artist of today, consciously or unconsciously, is indebted."

MEISSONIER

MEISSONIER

I never hesitate about scraping out the work of days, and beginning afresh, so as to satisfy myself, and try to do better. Ah! that " better " which one feels in one's soul, and without which no true artist is ever content! ¶ Others may approve and admire; but that counts for nothing, compared with one's own feeling of what ought to be.

—*Meissonier's Conversations*

MEISSONIER

LIFE in this world is a collecting, and all the men and women in it are collectors.

The question is, What will you collect? Most men are intent on collecting dollars. Their waking-hours are taken up with inventing plans, methods, schemes, whereby they may secure dollars from other men. To gather as many dollars as possible, and to give out as few, is the desideratum. But when you collect one thing you always incidentally collect others. The fisherman who casts his net for shad usually secures a few other fish, and once in a while a turtle, which enlarges the mesh to suit, and gives sweet liberty to the shad. To focus exclusively on dollars is to secure jealousy, fear, vanity, and a vaulting ambition that may claw its way through the mesh and let your dollars slip into the yeasty deep.

Ragged Haggard and his colleague, Cave-of-the-Winds, collect bacteria; while the fashionable young men of the day, with a few exceptions, are collecting headaches, regrets, weak nerves, tremens, paresis—death. Of course we shall all die (I will admit that), and further, we may be a long time dead (I will admit that), and moreover, we may be going through the world for the last time—as to that I do not know; but while we are

MEISSONIER

here it seems the part of reason to devote our energies to collecting that which brings as much quiet joy to ourselves, and as little annoyance to others, as possible.
¶ My heart goes out to the collector. In the soul of the collector of old books, swords, pistols, brocades, prints, clocks and bookplates, there is only truth. If he gives you his friendship, it is because you love the things that he loves; he has no selfish wish to use your good name to further his own petty plans—he only asks that you shall behold, and beholding, your eye shall glow, and your heart warm within you.
Inasmuch as we live in the age of the specialist, one man often collects books on only one subject, Dante for instance; another, nothing but volumes printed at Venice; another, works concerning the stage; and still another devotes all his spare time to securing tobacco-pipes. And I am well aware that the man who for a quarter of a century industriously collects snuffboxes has a supreme contempt for the man who collects both snuffboxes and clocks. And in this does the specialist reveal that his normal propensity to collect has degenerated. That is to say, it has refined itself into an abnormality, and from the innocent desire to collect, has shifted off into a selfish wish to outrival.
The man who collects many things, with easy, natural leanings toward, say, spoons, is pure in heart and free from guile; but when his soul centers on spoons exclusively, he has fallen from his high estate and is simply

MEISSONIER

possessed of a lust for ownership—he wants to own more peculiar spoons than any other man on earth. Such a one stirs up wrath and rivalry, and is the butt and byword of all others who collect spoons.

Prosperous, practical, busy people sometimes wonder why other folks build cabinets with glass fronts and strong locks and therein store postage-stamps, bits of old silks, autographs and books that are very precious only when their leaves are uncut; and so I will here endeavor to explain. At the same time I despair of making my words intelligible to any but those who are collectors, or mayhap to those others who are in the varioloid stage.

Then possibly you say I had better not waste good paper and ink by recording the information, since collectors know already, and those who are without the pale have neither eyes to see nor hearts to incline. But the simple fact is, the proposition that you comprehend on first hearing was yours already; for how can you recognize a thing as soon as it comes into view if you have never before seen it? You have thought my thought yourself, or else your heart would not beat fast and your lips say, " Yes, yes! " when I voice it. Truth is in the air, and when your head gets up into the right stratum of atmosphere you breathe it in. You may not know that you have breathed it in until I come along and write it out on this blank sheet, and then you read it and say, " Yes—your hand! that is surely so; I knew it

MEISSONIER

all along!" ¶ And so then if I tell you a thing you already know, I confer on you the great blessing of introducing you to yourself and of giving you the consciousness that you know.

And to know you know is power. And to feel the sense of power is to feel a sense of oneness with the Source of Power ⚜ ⚜

Let's see—what was it, then, that we were talking about? Oh, yes! collectors and collecting.

Men collect things because these things stir imagination and link them with the people who once possessed and used these things. Thus, through imagination, is the dead past made again to live and throb and pulse with life. Man is not the lonely creature that those folks with bad digestions sometimes try to have us believe.

We are brothers not only to all who live, but to all who have gone before.

And so we collect the trifles that once were valuables for other men, and by the possession of these trifles are we bounden to them. These things stimulate imagination, stir the sympathies, and help us forget the cramping bounds of time and space that so often hedge us close around ⚜ ⚜

The people near us may be sordid, stupid, mean; or more likely they are weary and worn with the battle for mere food, shelter and raiment; or they are depressed by that undefined brooding fear which civilization exacts as payment for benefits forgot—so their better

MEISSONIER

selves are subdued. ¶ But through fancy's flight we can pick our companions out of the company of saints and sinners who have long turned to dust. I have the bookplates of Holbein and Hogarth, and I have a book once owned by Rembrandt, and so I do not say Holbein and Hogarth and Rembrandt were—I say they are. And thus the collector confuses the glorious dead and the living in one fairy company; and although he may detect varying degrees of excellence, for none does he hold contempt, of none is he jealous, none does he envy. From them he asks nothing, upon him they make no demands. In the collector's cast of mind there is something very childlike and ingenuous.

My little girl has a small box of bright bits of silk thread that she hoards very closely; then she possesses certain pieces of calico, nails, curtain-rings, buttons, spools and fragments of china—all of which are very dear to her heart. And why should they not be? For with them she creates a fairy world, wherein are only joy, and peace, and harmony, and light—quite an improvement on this! Yes, dearie, quite.

MEISSONIER

RNEST MEISSONIER, the artist, began collecting very early. He has told us that he remembers, when five years of age, of going with his mother to market and collecting rabbits' ears and feet, which he would take home, and carefully nail up on the wall of the garret. And it may not be amiss to explain here that the rabbit's foot as an object of superstitious veneration has no real place outside of the United States of America, and this only south of Mason and Dixon's line.

The Meissonier lad's collection of rabbits' ears increased until he had nearly colors enough to run the chromatic scale. Then he collected pigeons' wings in like manner, and if you have ever haunted French market-places you know how natural a thing this would be for a child. The boy's mother took quite an interest in his amusements, and helped him to spread the wings out and arrange the tails fan-shape on the walls. They had long strings of buttons and boxes of spools in partnership; and when they would go up the Seine on little excursions on Sunday afternoons, they would bring back rich spoils in the way of swan feathers, butterflies, "snake-feeders" and tiny shells. Then once they found a bird's nest, and as the mother bird had deserted it, they carried it home. That was a red-letter day, for the garret collection had increased to such an extent that a partition was made across the corner of a room by hanging up a strip of cloth. And all the things in that

MEISSONIER

corner belonged to Ernest—his mother said so. Ernest's mother seems to have had a fine, joyous, childlike nature, so she fully entered into the life of her boy. He wanted no other companion. In fact, this mother was little better herself than a child in years—she was only sixteen when she bore him. They lived at Lyons then, but three years later moved to Paris. Her temperament was poetic, religious, and her spirit had in it a touch of superstition—which is the case with all really excellent women ♜ ♜

But this sweet playtime was not for long—the mother died in Eighteen Hundred Twenty-five, aged twenty-four years.

I suppose there is no greater calamity that can befall a child than to lose his mother. Still, Nature is very kind, and for Ernest Meissonier there always remained firm, clear-cut memories of a slight, fair-haired woman, with large, open, gray eyes, who held him in her arms, sang to him, and rocked him to sleep each night as the darkness gathered. He lived over and over again those few sunshiny excursions up the river; and he knew all the reeds and flowers and birds she liked best, and the places where they had landed from the boat and lunched together were forever to him sacred spots.

But the death of his mother put a stop for a time to his collecting. The sturdy housekeeper who came to take the mother's place, speedily cleared " the truck " out of the corner, and forbade the bringing of any more

MEISSONIER

feathers and rabbits' feet into her house—well, I guess so! The birds' nests, long grasses, reeds, shells and pigeons' wings were tossed straightway into the fireplace, and went soaring up the chimney in smoke.

The destruction of the collection did n't kill the propensity to collect, however, any more than you can change a man's opinions by burning his library. It only dampened the desire for a time. It broke out again after a few years and continued for considerably more than half a century. There was a house at Poissy " full to the roof-tiles " of books, marbles, bronzes and innumerable curios, gathered from every corner of the earth; and a palace at Paris filled in like manner, for which Ernest Meissonier had expended more than a million francs.

In the palace at Paris, when the owner was near his threescore years and ten, he took from a locker a morocco case, and opening it, showed his friend, Dumas, a long curl of yellow hair; and then he brought out a curious old white-silk dress, and said to the silent Dumas, " This curl was cut from my mother's head after her death, and this dress was her wedding-gown."

¶ A few days after this Meissonier wrote these words in his journal: " It is the Twentieth of February—the morning of my seventieth birthday. What a long time to look back upon! This morning, at the hour when my mother gave me birth, I wished my first thoughts to be of her. Dear Mother, how often have the tears risen

MEISSONIER

to my eyes at the remembrance of you! It was your absence—the longing I had for you—that made you so dear to me. The love of my heart goes out to you! Do you hear me, Mother, calling and crying for you? How sweet it must be to have a mother, I say to myself."

MEISSONIER

"I WOULD have every man rich," said Emerson, "that he might know the worthlessness of riches."
Every man should have a college education, in order to show him how little the thing is really worth. The intellectual kings of the earth have seldom been college-bred. Napoleon ever regretted the lack of instruction in his early years; and in the minds of such men as Abraham Lincoln and Ernest Meissonier there usually lingers the suspicion that they have dropped something out of their lives.

"I'm not a college man—ask Seward," said Lincoln, when some one questioned him as to the population of Alaska. The remark was merry jest, of course, but as in all jest there lurks a grain of truth, so did there here ※
At the height of Meissonier's success, when a canvas from his hand commanded a larger price than the work of any other living artist, he exclaimed, "Oh, if only I had been given the advantages of a college training!"
¶If he had, it is quite probable that he never would have painted better than his teacher. Discipline might have reduced his daring genius to neutral salts, and taken all that fine audacity from his brush.

He was a natural artist: he saw things clearly and in detail; he had the heart to feel, and he longed for the skill to express that which he saw and felt. And when the desire is strong enough it brings the thing—and thus is prayer answered.

MEISSONIER

Meissonier while but a child set to work making pictures —he declared he would be an artist. And in spite of his father's attempts to shame him out of his whim, and to starve him into a more practical career, his resolution stuck ❧ ❧
He worked in a drugstore and drew on the wrapping-paper; then with this artist a few days, and then with that. He tried illustrating, and finally a bold stand was made and a little community formed that decided on storming the Salon.
There is something pathetic in that brotherhood of six young men, binding themselves together, swearing they would stand together and aid each other in producing great art.
The dead seriousness of the scheme has a peculiar sophomore quality. There were Steinheil, Trimolet, Daumier, Daubigny, Deschaumaes and Meissonier, all aged about twenty, strong, sturdy, sincere and innocently ignorant—all bound they would be artists.
Two of these young men were sign-painters, the others did odd jobs illustrating, and filled in the time at anything which chance offered. When one got an invitation out to dinner he would go, and furtively drop biscuit and slices of meat into his lap, and then slyly transfer them to his waistcoat-pockets, so as to take them to his less fortunate brethren.
They haunted the galleries, made themselves familiar with catalogs, criticized without stint, knew all about

MEISSONIER

current prices, and were able to point out the great artists of Paris when they passed proudly up the street.
¶ They sketched eternally, formed small wax models, and made great preparations for masterpieces.

The reason they did not produce the masterpieces was because they did not have money to buy brushes, paints and canvas. Neither did they have funds to purchase food to last until the thing was done; and it is difficult to produce great art on half-rations. So they formed the brotherhood, and one midnight swore eternal fealty. They were to draw lots: the lucky member was to paint and the other five were to support him for a month. He was to be supplied his painting outfit and to be absolutely free from all responsibility as to the bread-and-butter question for a whole month.

Trimolet was the first lucky man.

He set diligently to work, and dined each evening on a smoking mutton-chop with a bottle of wine, at a respectable restaurant. The five stood outside and watched him through the window—they dined when and where they could.

His picture grew apace, and in three weeks was completed. It was entitled, " Sisters of Charity Giving Out Soup to the Poor." The work was of a good machine-made quality, not good enough to praise nor bad enough to condemn: it was like Tomlinson of Berkeley Square.
¶ On account of the peculiar subject with which it dealt, it found favor with a worthy priest, who bought

MEISSONIER

it and presented it to a convent. ¶ This so inflated Trimolet that he suggested it would be a good plan to keep right on with the arrangement, but the five objected ✠ ✠
Steinheil was next appointed to feed the vestal fire. His picture was so-so, but would not sell.
Daubigny came next, and lived so high that inspiration got clogged, fatty degeneration of the cerebrum set in, and after a week he ceased to paint—doing nothing but dream ✠ ✠
When the turn of the fourth man came, Meissonier had concluded that the race must be won by one and one, and his belief in individualism was further strengthened by an order for a group of family portraits, with a goodly retainer in advance.
Straightway he married Steinheil's sister, with whom he had been some weeks in love, and the others feeling aggrieved that an extra mouth to feed, with danger of more, had been added to the "Commune," declared the compact void.
Trimolet still thought well of the arrangement, though, and agreed, if Meissonier would support him, to secure fame and fortune for them both.
Meissonier declined the offer with thanks, and struck boldly out on his own account.
The woman who had so recklessly agreed to share his poverty must surely have had faith in him—or are very young people who marry incapable of either faith

MEISSONIER

or reason? Never mind; she did not hold the impulsive young man back.

She could n't—nothing but death could have stayed such ambition. His will was unbending and his ambition never tired.

He was an athlete in strength, and was fully conscious that to be a good animal is the first requisite. He swam, rowed, walked, and could tire out any of his colleagues at swordplay or skittles.

But material things were scarce those first few years of married life, and once when the table had bread, but no meat nor butter, he took the entire proceeds of a picture and purchased a suit of clothing of the time of Louis the Grand: not to wear, of course—simply to put in the "collection."

Small wonder is it that, for some months after, when he would walk out alone the fond wife would caution him thus: "Now Ernest, do not go through that old-clothes market—you know your weakness."

"I have no money, so you need not worry," he would gaily reply.

Of those times of pinching want he has written, "As to happiness—is it possible to be wretched at twenty, when one has health, a passion for art, free passes for the Louvre, an eye to see, a heart to feel, and sunshine gratis?"

But poverty did not last long. Pictures such as this young man produced must attract attention anywhere.

MEISSONIER

He belonged to no school, but simply worked away after his own fashion; what he was bound to do was to produce a faithful picture—sure, clear, strong, vivid. He saw things clearly and his sympathies were acute, as is shown in every canvas he produced.

Meissonier had the true artistic conscience—he was incapable of putting out an average, unobjectionable picture—it must have positive excellence. " There is a difference," said he, " between a successful effort and a work of love." He painted only in the loving mood.

¶ No greater blessing than the artistic conscience can come to any worker in art, be he sculptor, writer, singer or painter. Hold fast to it, and it shall be your compass in time when the sun is darkened. To please the public is little, but to satisfy your Other Self, that self that leans over your shoulder and watches your every thought and deed, is much. No artistic success worth having is possible unless you satisfy that Other Self But like the moral conscience it can be dallied with until the grieved spirit turns away, and the wretch is left to his fate.

Meissonier never hesitated to erase a whole picture when it did not satisfy his inward sense—customers might praise and connoisseurs offer to buy, it made no difference. " I have some one who is more difficult to please than you," he would say; " I must satisfy myself."

¶ The fine intoxication that follows good artistic work is the highest joy that mortals ever know. But once let

MEISSONIER

a creative artist lower his standard and give the world the mere product of his brain, with heart left out, that man will hate himself for a year and a day. He has sold his soul for a price: joy has flown, and bitterness is his portion. Meissonier never trifled with his compass. To the last he headed for the polestar.

MEISSONIER

HE early domestic affairs of Meissonier can best be guessed from his oft-repeated assertion that the artist should never marry. " To produce great work, Art must be your mistress," he said. " You must be married to your work. A wife demands unswerving loyalty as her right, and a portion of her husband's time she considers her own. This is proper with every profession but that of Art. The artist must not be restrained, nor should even a wife come between him and his Art. The artist must not be judged by the same standards that are made for other men. Why? Simply because when you begin to tether him you cramp his imagination and paralyze his hand. The priest and artist must not marry, for it is too much to expect any woman to follow them in their flight, and they have no moral right to tie themselves to a woman and then ask her to stay behind."
¶ From this and many similar passages in the " Conversations " it is clear that Meissonier had no conception of the fact that a woman may possibly keep step with her mate. He simply never considered such a thing ⚜ ⚜
A man's opinions concerning womankind are based upon the knowledge of the women he knows best.
We can not apply Hamerton's remark concerning Turner to Meissonier. Hamerton said that throughout Turner's long life he was lamentably unfortunate in that he never came under the influence of a strong and

MEISSONIER

good woman. ¶ Meissonier associated with good women, but he never knew one with a spread of spiritual wing sufficient to fit her to be his companion. There is a minor key of loneliness and heart hunger running through his whole career. Possibly, in the wisdom of Providence, this was just what he needed to urge him on to higher and nobler ends. He never knew peace, and the rest for which he sighed slipped him at the very last. "I'm tired, so tired," he sighed again and again in those later years, when he had reached the highest pinnacle. ¶ And still he worked—it was his only rest! Meissonier painted very few pictures of women, and in some miraculous way skipped that stage in esthetic evolution wherein most artists affect the nude. In his whole career he never produced a single "Diana," nor a "Susanna at the Bath." He had no artistic sympathy with "Leda and the Swan," and once when Delaroche chided him for painting no pictures of women, he was so ungallant as to say, "My dear fellow, men are much more beautiful than women!"

During the last decade of his life Meissonier painted but one portrait of a woman, and to America belongs the honor. The sitter was Mrs. J. W. Mackay, of California. ¶ As all the world knows, Mrs. Mackay refused to accept the canvas. She declared the picture was no likeness, and further, she would not have it for a gift ⚜ "So you do not care for the picture?" asked the great artist. ¶ "Me? Well, I guess not—not that picture!"

MEISSONIER

¶ "Very well, Madam. I think—I think I'll keep it for myself. I'll place it on exhibition!" And the great artist looked out of the window in an absent-minded way, and hummed a tune.

This put another phase on the matter. Mrs. Mackay winced, and paid the price, which rumor says was somewhere between ten and twenty-five thousand dollars. She took the little canvas in her carriage and drove away with it, and what became of the only portrait of a woman painted by Meissonier during his later years, nobody knew but Mrs. Mackay, and Mrs. Mackay never told.

Meissonier once explained to a friend that his offense consisted in producing a faithful likeness of the customer.
¶ The Mackay incident did not end when the lady paid the coin and accepted the goods. Meissonier, by the haughtiness of his manner, his artistic independence, and most of all, by his unpardonable success, had been sowing dragons' teeth for half a century. And now armed enemies sprang up, and sided with the woman from California. They made it an international episode: less excuses have involved nations in war in days agone. But the enemies of Meissonier did not belong alone to America, although here every arm was braced and every tongue wagged to vindicate the cause of our countrywoman ❦ ❦

In Paris the whole art world was divided into those who sided with Meissonier and those who were against him.

MEISSONIER

Cafes echoed with the sounds of wordy warfare; the columns of all magazines and newspapers bulged with heated argument; newsboys cried extras on the street, and bands of students paraded the boulevards singing songs in praise of Mrs. Mackay and in dishonor of Meissonier, " the pretender." The assertion was made again and again that Meissonier had fed sham art upon the public, and by means of preposterous prices and noisy puffing had hypnotized a world. They called him the artist of the Infinitely Little, King of Lilliput, and challenged any one to show where he had thrown heart and high emotion into his work. Studies of coachmen, smokers, readers, soldiers, housemaids, chess-players, cavaliers and serenaders were not enough upon which to base an art reputation—the man must show that he had moved men to high endeavor, said the detractors. A fund was started to purchase the Mackay portrait, so as to do the very thing that Meissonier had threatened to do, but dare not: place the picture on exhibition. To show the picture, the enemy said, would be to prove the artist's commonplace quality, and not only this, but it would prove the man a rogue. They declared he was incapable of perceiving the good qualities in a sitter, and had consented for a price to portray a person whom he disliked; and as a result, of course, had produced a caricature; and then had blackmailed his patron into paying an outrageous sum to keep the picture from the public.

MEISSONIER

The argument sounded plausible. And so the battle raged, just as it has since in reference to Zola.

The tide of Meissonier's prosperity began to ebb: prospective buyers kept away; those who had given commissions canceled them.

Meissonier's friends saw that something must be done. They inaugurated a "Meissonier Vindication," by making an exhibition of one hundred fifty-five " Meissoniers "—and the public was invited to come and be the jury. Art-lovers from England went in bodies, and all Paris filed through the gallery, as well as a goodly portion of provincial France. By the side of each canvas stood a gendarme to protect it from a possible fanatic whose artistic hate could not be restrained.

To a great degree this exhibition brought feeling to a normal condition. Meissonier was still a great artist, yet he was human and his effects were now believed to be gotten by natural methods. But there was a lull in the mad rush to secure his wares. The Vanderbilts grew lukewarm; titled connoisseurs from England were not so anxious; and Mrs. Mackay sat back and smiled through her tears.

Meissonier had expended over a million francs on his house in the Boulevard Malesherbes in Paris, and nearly as much on the country-seat at Poissy. These places were kingly in their appointments and such as only the State should attempt to maintain. For a single man, by the work of his right hand, to keep them up was too

MEISSONIER

much to expect. ¶ Meissonier's success had been too great. As a collector he had overdone the thing. Only poor men, or those of moderate incomes, should be collectors, for then the joy of sacrifice is theirs. Charles Lamb's covetous looking on the book when it was red, daily for months, meanwhile hoarding his pay, and at last one Saturday night swooping down and carrying the volume home to Bridget in triumph, is the true type. ¶ But money had come to Meissonier by hundreds of thousands of francs, and often sums were forced upon him as advance payments. He lived royally and never imagined that his hand and brain could lose their cunning, or the public be fickle.

The fact that a " vindication " had been necessary was galling: the great man grew irritable and his mood showed itself in his work: his colors grew hard and metallic, and there were angles in his lines where there should have been joyous curves.

Debts began to press. He painted less and busied his mind with reminiscence—the solace of old age.

And then it was that he dictated to his wife the " Conversations." The book reveals the quality of his mind with rare fidelity—and shows the power of this second wife fully to comprehend him. Thus did she disprove some of the unkind philosophy given to the world by her liege. But the talk in the " Conversations " is of an old man in whose heart was a tinge of bitterness. Yet the thought is often lofty and the comment clear and

MEISSONIER

full of flashing insight. It is the book of Ecclesiastes over again, written in a minor key, with a little harmless gossip added for filling. Meissonier died in Paris on the Twenty-first of January, Eighteen Hundred Ninety-one, aged seventy-six years.

MEISSONIER

HE canvas known as "Eighteen Hundred Seven," which is regarded as Meissonier's masterpiece, has a permanent home in the Metropolitan Museum of Art in New York. The central figure is Napoleon, at whose shrine the great artist loved to linger. The "Eighteen Hundred Seven" occupied the artist's time and talent for fifteen years, and was purchased by A. T. Stewart for sixty thousand dollars. After Mr. Stewart's death his art treasures were sold at auction, and this canvas was bought by Judge Henry Hilton and presented to the city of New York.

There are in all about seventy-five pictures by Meissonier owned in America. Several of his pieces are in the Vanderbilt collection, others are owned by collectors in Chicago, Cleveland and Saint Louis.

There are various glib sayings to the effect that the work of great men is not appreciated until after they are dead. This may be so and it may not. It depends upon the man and the age. Meissonier enjoyed full half a century of the highest and most complete success that was ever bestowed upon an artist.

The strong intellect and marked personality of the man won him friends wherever he chose to make them; and it probably would have been better for his art if a degree of public indifference had been his portion in those earlier years. His success was too great: the calm judgment of posterity can never quite endorse the plaudits

MEISSONIER

paid the living man. He is one of the greatest artists the Nineteenth Century has produced, but that his name can rank among the great artists of all time is not at all probable.

William Michael Rossetti has summed the matter up well by saying: " Perfection is so rare in this world that when we find it we must pause and pay it the tribute of our silent admiration. It is very easy to say that Meissonier should have put in this and omitted that. Had he painted differently he would have been some one else. The work is faultless, and such genius as he showed must ever command the homage of those who know by experience the supreme difficulty of having the hand materialize the conceptions of the mind. And yet Meissonier's conceptions outmatched his brush: he was greater than his work. He was a great artist, and better still, a great man—proud, frank, fearless and conscientious." ❧ ❧

TITIAN

TITIAN

Titian by a few strokes of the brush knew how to make the general image and character of whatever object he attempted. His great care was to preserve the masses of light and of shade, and to give by opposition the idea of that solidity which is inseparable from natural objects. He was the greatest of the Venetians, and deserves to rank with Raphael and Michelangelo.

—*Sir Joshua Reynolds*

TITIAN

THE march of progress and the rage for improvement make small impression on Venice. The cabmen have not protested against horsecars as they did in Rome, tearing up the tracks, mobbing the drivers, and threatening the passengers; neither has the cable superseded horses as a motor power, and the trolley then rendered the cable obsolete.

In short, there never was a horse in Venice, save those bronze ones over the entrance to Saint Mark's, and the one Napoleon rode to the top of the Campanile. But there are lions in Venice—stone lions—you see them at every turn. "Did you ever see a live horse?" asked a ten-year-old boy of me, in Saint Mark's Square.

"Yes," said I; "several times."

"Are they fierce?" he asked after a thoughtful pause. And then I explained that a thousand times as many men are killed by horses every year as by lions.

Four hundred years have made no change in the style of gondolas, or anything else in Venice. The prow of the Venetian gondola made today is of the same height as that prescribed by Tommaso Mocenigo, Doge in the year Fourteen Hundred. The regulated height of the prow is to insure protection for the passengers when

TITIAN

going under bridges, but its peculiar halberd shape is a thing not one of the five thousand gondoliers in Venice can explain. If you ask your gondolier he will swear a pious oath, shrug his fine shoulders, and say, " Mon Dieu, Signore! how should I know?—it has always been so." The ignorance and superstition of the picturesque gondolier, with his fluttering blue hatband and gorgeous sash, are most enchanting. His lack of knowledge is like the ignorance of childhood, when life has neither beginning nor end; when ways and means present no vexatious problems; when if food is not to be had for the simple asking, it can surely be secured by coaxing; when the day is for frolic and play, and the night for dreams and sleep.

But although your gondolier may not be able to read or write, he yet has his preferences in music and art, and possesses definite ideas as to the eternal fitness of things. In Italy, many of the best paintings being in churches, and all the galleries being free on certain days, the common people absorb a goodly modicum of art education without being aware of it. I have heard marketwomen compare the merits of Tintoretto and Paul Veronese, and stupid indeed is the boat " hooker " in Venice who would not know a " Titian " on sight.

But the chronology of art is all a jumble to this indolent, careless, happy people. These paintings were in the churches when their fathers and mothers were alive, they are here now, and no church has been built in

TITIAN

Venice for three hundred years ❧ The history of Venice is nothing to a gondolier. " Why, Signore! how should I know? Venice always has been," explained Enrico, when I asked him how old the city was. ¶ When I hired Enrico I thought he was a youth. He wore such a dandy suit of pure white, and his hatband so exactly matched his sash, that I felt certain I was close upon some tender romance, for surely it was some dark-eyed lacemaker who had embroidered this impossible hatband and evolved the improbable sash!
The exercise of rowing a gondola is of the sort that gives a splendid muscular development. Men who pull oars have round shoulders, but the gondolier does not pull an oar, he pushes it, and as a result has a flat back and brawny chest. Enrico had these, and as he had no nerves to speak of, the passing years had taken small toll. Enrico was sixty. Once he ran alongside another gondola and introduced me to the gondolier, who was his son. They were both of one age. Then one day I went with Enrico to his home—two whitewashed rooms away up under the roof of an old palace on the Rialto—and there met his wife.
Mona Lisa showed age more than Enrico. She had crouched over a little wooden frame making one pattern of lace for thirty years, so her form was bent and her eyesight fautly. Yet she proudly explained that years and years ago she was a model for a painter, and in the Della Salute I could see her picture, posed as

TITIAN

Magdalen. She got fourteen cents a day for her work, and had been at it so long she had no desire to quit. She took great pride in Enrico's white-duck suits and explained to me that she never let him wear one suit more than two days without its being washed and starched; and she always pipeclayed his shoes and carefully inspected him each morning before sending him forth to his day's work. "Men are so careless, you know," she added by way of apology.

There was no furniture in the rooms worth mentioning —Italians do not burden themselves with things—but on the wall I caught sight of a bright-colored unfinished sketch of the Bridge of Sighs. It was little more than an outline, and probably did not represent ten minutes' work, but the lines seemed so firm and sure that I at once asked who did it.

"An American did it, Signore, an American painter; he comes here every year; our son is his gondolier and shows him all the best places to paint, and takes him there when the light is good and keeps the people back so the artist can work—you understand? A shower came up just as his Excellency, the American, began on this, and it got wet and so he gave it to my son and he gave it to me."

"What is the painter's name?" I asked. Enrico could not remember, but Mona Lisa said his name was Signore Hopsmithiziano, or something like that.

There were several little plaster images on the walls,

TITIAN

and through the open door that led to the adjoining room I saw a sort of an improvised shrine, with various little votive offerings grouped about an unframed canvas. The picture was a crude attempt at copying that grand figure in Titian's "Assumption." ¶ "And who painted that?" I asked.
Enrico crossed himself in silence, and Mona Lisa's subdued voice answered: "Our other son did that. He was only nineteen. He was a mosaicist and was studying to be a painter; he was drowned at the Lido."
The old woman made the sign of the cross, her lips moved, and a single big tear stood on her leathery cheek. I changed the painful subject, and soon found excuse to slip away. That evening as the darkness gathered and twinkling lights began to appear like fireflies, up and down the Grand Canal, I sat in a little balcony of my hotel watching the scene. A serenading party, backing their boats out into the stream, had formed a small blockade, and in the group of gondolas that awaited the unraveling of the tangle I spied Enrico. He had a single passenger, a lady in the inevitable black mantilla, holding in her hands the inevitable fan. A second glance at the lady—and sure enough! it was Mona Lisa. I ran downstairs, stepped out across the moored line of gondolas, took up a hook, and reaching over gently pulled Enrico's gondola over so I could step aboard.
Mona Lisa was crooning a plaintive love-song and her gondolier was coming in occasionally with bars of

TITIAN

melodious bass. I felt guilty for being about to break in upon such a sentimental little scene, and was going to retreat, but Enrico and Mona Lisa spied me and both gave a little cry of surprise and delight.
"Where have you been?" I asked—"you fine old lovers!" ✄ ✄
And then they explained that it was a Holy Day and they had been over to the Church of San Giorgio, and were now on their way to Santa Maria de' Frari.
" It is a very special mass, by torchlight, and is for the repose of the soul of Titian, who is buried there. You may never have an opportunity to see such a sight again—come with us," and Enrico held out his strong brown hand.
I stepped aboard, the boats opened out to the left and to the right, and we passed with that peculiar rippling sound, across the water that reflected the lights as of a myriad stars.

TITIAN

TITIAN was born one hundred years before Rubens, and died just six months before Rubens' birth.

On the one hundred twenty-second anniversary of the birth of Titian, Rubens knelt at his grave, there in the church of Santa Maria de' Frari, and vowed he would follow in the footsteps of the illustrious master. And the next day he wrote to his mother describing the incident. Thousands of other sentimental and impulsive youth have stood before that little slab of black marble on which is carved the simple legend, "Tiziano Vecellio," and vowed as Rubens did, but out of the throng not one rendered such honor to the master as did the brilliant Fleming. The example of Titian was a lifelong inspiration to Rubens; and to all his pupils he held up Titian as the painter par excellence. In the Rubens studio Titian was the standard by which all art was gauged.

When Rubens returned to Flanders from Italy he carried with him twenty-one pictures done by the hand of the master.

Titian was born at the little village of Cadore, a few miles north of Venice. When ten years of age his father took him down to the city and apprenticed him to a worker in mosaic, the intent of the fond parent probably being to get the youngster out of the way, more than anything else.

The setting together of the little bits of colored glass,

TITIAN

according to a pattern supplied, is a task so simple that children can do it about as well as grown folks. They do the work there today just exactly as they did four hundred years ago, when little Tiziano Vecellio came down from Cadore and worked, getting his ears pinched when he got sleepy, or carelessly put in the red glass when he should have used the blue.

An inscription on a tomb at Beni Hassan, dating from the reign of Osortasen the First, who lived three thousand years before Christ, represents Theban glassblowers at work. I told Enrico of this one day when we were on our way to a glass-factory.

"That's nothing," said Enrico; "it was the glassblowers of Venice who taught them how," and not a ghost of a smile came across his fine, burnt-umber face.

¶ There is a story by Pliny about certain Phenician mariners landing on the shores of a small river in Palestine and making a fire to cook their food, and afterward discovering that the soda and sand under their pots had fused into glass. No one now seriously considers that the first discovery of glass, and for all I know Enrico may be right in his flat statement that the first glass was made at Venice, " for Venice always was."

The art of glassmaking surely goes back to the morning of the world. The glassblower is a classic, like the sower who goes forth to sow, the potter at his wheel, and the grinding of grain with mortar and pestle. Thus, too, the

TITIAN

art of the mosaicist—who places bright bits of stone and glass in certain positions so as to form a picture—goes back to the dawn. The exquisite work in mosaic at Pompeii is the first thing that impresses the visitor to that silent city. Much of the work there was done long before the Christian era, and must have then been practised many centuries to bring it to such perfection.
¶ Young Tiziano from Cadore did not like the mere following of a set pattern—he introduced variations of his own, and got his nose tweaked for trying to improve on a good thing. Altogether he seemed to have had a hard time of it there at Messer Zuccato's mosaic-shop.
¶ The painter's art, then as now, preceded the art of the mosaicist, for the picture or design to be made in mosaic is first carefully drawn on paper, and then colored, and the worker in mosaic is supposed simply to follow copy. When you visit the glass-factories of Venice today, you see the painted picture tacked up on the wall before the workmen, who with deft fingers stick the bits of glass into their beds of putty. This scheme of painting a pattern is in order that cheap help can be employed; when it began we do not know, but we do know there was a time when the great artist in mosaic had his design in his head, and materialized it by rightly placing the bits of glass with his own hands, experimenting, selecting and rejecting until the thing was right. But this was before the time of Titian, for when Titian came down to Venice there were painters

TITIAN

employed in the shop of Sebastian Zuccato who made the designs for the dunderheads to follow. That is not just the word the painters used to designate the boys and women who placed the bits of glass in position, but it meant the same thing.

The painters thought themselves great folks, and used to make the others wait on them and run errands, serving them as " fags."

But the Vecellio boy did not worship at the shrine of the painters who made the designs. He said he could make as good pictures himself, and still continued to make changes in the designs when he thought they should be made; and once in a dispute between the boy and the maker of a design, the master took sides with the boy. This inflated the lad with his own importance so, that shortly after he applied for the position of the quarrelsome designer.

The fine audacity of the youngster so pleased the master that he allowed him to try his hand with the painters a few hours each day. He was getting no wages anyway, only his board, and the kind of board did not cost much, so it did not make much difference.

In Venice at that time there were two painters by the name of Bellini—Gentile and Giovanni, sons of the painter Jacob Bellini, who had brought his boys up in the way they should go. Gian, as the Venetians called the younger brother, was the more noted of the two. Occasionally he made designs for the mosaicists, and

TITIAN

this sometimes brought him to the shop where young Titian worked.

The boy got on speaking terms with the great painter, and ran errands back and forth from his studio. When twelve years of age we find him duly installed as a helper at Gian Bellini's studio, with an easel and box of paints all his own.

TITIAN

HE brightest scholar in the studio of Gian Bellini was a young man by the name of Giorgio, but they called him Giorgione, which being interpreted means George the Great. He was about the age of Titian, and the two became firm friends.

Giorgione was nearly twenty when we first hear of him. He was a handsome fellow—tall, slender, with an olive complexion and dreamy brown eyes. There was a becoming flavor of melàncholy in his manner, and more than one gracious dame sought to lure him back to earth, away from his sadness, out of the dream-world in which he lived.

Giorgione was a musician and a poet. He sang his own pieces, playing the accompaniment on a harp. Vasari says he sang his songs, playing his own accompaniment on a flute, but I think this is a mistake.

Into all his work Giorgione infused his own soul—and do you know what the power to do that is? It is genius. To be able to make a statue is little, but to breathe into its nostrils the breath of life—ah! that is something else! The last elusive, undefinable stroke of the brush, that something uniting the spirit of the beholder with the spirit of the artist, so that you feel as he felt when he wrought—that is art. Burne-Jones is the avatar of Giorgione. He subdues you into silence, and you wait, expecting that one of his tall, soulful dream-women will speak, if you are but worthy—holding your soul in

TITIAN

tune. ¶ Giorgione never wrought so well as Burne-Jones, because he lived in a different age—all art is an evolution. Painting is a form of expression, just as language is a form of expression. Every man who writes English is debtor to Shakespeare. Every man who paints and expresses something of that which his soul feels is debtor to Giorgione and Botticelli. But to judge of the greatness of an artist—mind this—you must compare him with his contemporaries, not with those who were before or those who came after. The old masters are valuable, not necessarily for beauty, but because they reveal the evolution of art.

Between Burne-Jones and Giorgione came Botticelli. Now, Botticelli builded on Giorgione, while Burne-Jones builded on Botticelli. Aubrey Beardsley, dead at the age at which Keats died, builded on both, but he perverted their art and put a leer where Burne-Jones placed faith and abiding trust. Aubrey Beardsley got the cue for his hothouse art from one figure in Botticelli's "Spring." I need not state which figure: a glance at the picture and you behold sulphur fumes about the face of one of the women.

Did Aubrey Beardsley infuse his own spirit into his work? Yes, I think he did. Mrs. Jameson says, "There are no successful imitations of Giorgione, neither can there be, for the spirit of the man is in every face he drew, and the people who try to draw like him always leave that out."

TITIAN

There are various pictures in the Louvre, the National Gallery, and the Pinacothek at Munich, signed with Giorgione's name, but Mrs. Jameson declares they are not his, " because they do not speak to your soul with that mild, beseeching look of pity." Possibly we should make allowance for Mrs. Jameson's warm praise—other women talked like that when Giorgione was alive.
Giorgione was one of those bright luminaries that dart across our plane of vision and then go out quickly in hopeless night, leaving only the memory of a blinding light. He died at thirty-three, which Disraeli declares is the age at which the world's saviors have usually died—and he names the Redeemer first in a list of twenty who passed out at the age of three-and-thirty. Disraeli does not say that all those in his list were saviors, for the second name he records is that of Alexander the Great, the list ending with Shelley.
Giorgione died of a broken heart ✄ The girl he loved eloped with his friend, Morta del Feltri, to whom he had proudly introduced her a short time before. It is an old story—it has been played again and again to its Da Rimini finish. The friend introduces the friend, and the lauded virtues of this friend inflames imagination, until love strikes a spark; then soon instead of three we find one—one groping blindly, alone, dazed, stunned, bereft ✄ ✄
The handsome Giorgione pined away, refusing to be comforted. And soon his proud, melancholy soul took

TITIAN

its flight from an environment with which he was ever at war, and from a world which he never loved. And Titian was sent for to complete the pictures which he had begun.

Surely, disembodied spirits have no control over mortals, or the soul of Giorgione would have come back and smitten the hand of Titian with palsy.

For a full year before he died Giorgione had not spoken to Titian, although he had seen him daily.

Giorgione had surpassed all artists in Venice. He had a careless, easy, limpid style. But there was decision and surety in his swinging lines, and best of all, a depth of tenderness and pity in his faces that gave to the whole a rich, full and melting harmony.

Giorgione's head touched heaven, and his feet were not always on earth. Titian's feet were always on earth, and his head sometimes touched heaven. Titian was healthy and in love with this old, happy, cruel, sensuous world. He was willing to take his chances anywhere. He had no quarrel with his environment, for did he not stay here a hundred years (lacking half a year), and then die through accident? Of course he liked it. One woman, for him, could make a paradise in which a thousand nightingales sang. And if one particular woman liked some one else better, he just consoled himself with the thought that " there is just as good fish," etc. I will not quote Walt Whitman and say his feet were tenoned and mortised in granite, but they were well planted on the

TITIAN

soil—and sometimes mired in clay. ¶ Titian admired Giorgione; he admired him so much that he painted exactly like him—or as nearly as he could.

Titian was a good-looking young man, but he was not handsome like Giorgione. Yet Titian did his best; he patronized Giorgione's tailor, imitated his dreamy, far-away look, used a brush with his left hand, and painted with his thumb. His coloring was the same, and when he got a commission to fresco the ceiling of a church he did it as nearly like Giorgione frescoes as he could

This kind of thing is not necessarily servile imitation—it is only admiration tipped to t' other side. It is found everywhere in aspiring youth and in every budding artist

As in the animal kingdom, genius has its prototype. In the National Gallery at London you will see in the Turner Room a "Claude Lorraine" and a "Turner" hung side by side, as provided for in Turner's will. You would swear, were the pictures not labeled, that one hand did them both. When thirty, Turner admired Claude to a slavish degree; but we know there came a time when he bravely set sail on a chartless sea, and left the great Claude Lorraine far astern.

Titian loved Giorgione so well that he even imitated his faults. At first this high compliment was pleasing to Giorgione; then he became indifferent, and finally disgusted. The very sight of Titian gave him a pain.

TITIAN

He avoided his society. He ceased to speak to him when they met, and forbade his friends to mention the name " Titian " in his presence.

It was about this time that Giorgione's ladylove won fame by discarding him in that foolish, fishwife fashion. He called his attendants and instructed them thus: " Do not allow that painter from Cadore—never mind his name—to attend my funeral—you understand? "

¶ Then he turned his face to the wall and died.

In his studio were various pictures partly completed, for it seems to have been his habit to get rest by turning from one piece of work to another. His executors looked at these unfinished canvases in despair. There was only one man in all Venice who could complete them, and that was Titian.

Titian was sent for.

He came, completed the pictures, signed them with the dead man's name, and gave them to the world.

" And," says the veracious Vasari, " they were done just as well, if not better than Giorgione himself could have done them, had he been alive! "

It was absurd of Giorgione to die of a broken heart and let Titian come in, making free with everything in his studio, and complete his work. It was very absurd.

Time is the great avenger—let us wait. Morta del Feltri, the perfidious friend, grew tired of his mistress: their love was so warm it shortly burned itself to ashes—ashes of roses.

TITIAN

Morta deserted the girl, fled from Venice, joined the army, and a javelin plunged through his liver at the battle of Zara ended his career.

The unhappy young woman, twice a widow, fought off hungry wolves by finding work in a glass-factory, making mosaics at fourteen cents a day. When she was seventy, Titian, aged seventy-five, painted her picture as a beggar-woman.

TITIAN

HE quality of sentiment that clings about the life of Giorgione seems to forbid a cool, critical view of his work. Byron indited a fine poem to him; and poetic criticism seems for him the proper kind. The glamour of sentiment conceals the real man from our sight. And anyway, it is hardly good manners to approach a saint closely and examine his halo to see whether it be genuine or not. Halos are much more beautiful when seen through the soft, mellow light of distance.

Giorgione's work was mostly in fresco, so but little of it has survived. But of his canvases several surely have that tender, beseeching touch of spirit which stamps the work as great art.

Whether Mrs. Jameson is right in her assumption that all canvases bearing Giorgione's name are spurious which lack that look of pity, is a question. I think that Mrs. Jameson is more kind than critical, although my hope is that Renan is correct in his gratuitous statement, "At the Last Great Day men will be judged by women, and the Almighty will merely vise the verdict." If this be true, all who, like Giorgione, have died for the love of woman will come off lightly.

But the fact is, no man is great all the time. Genius is an exceptional mood even in a genius, and happy is the genius who, like Tennyson, builds a high wall about his house, so he is seen but seldom, and destroys most of his commonplace work.

TITIAN

Ruskin has printed more rubbish than literature—ten times over. I have his complete works, and am sorry to say that, instead of confining myself to "Sesame and Lilies," I have foolishly read all the dreary stuff, including statistics, letters to Hobbs and Nobbs, with hot arguments as to who fished the murex up, and long, scathing tirades against the old legal shark who did him out of a hundred pounds. Surely, to be swindled by a lawyer is not so unusual a thing that it is worth recording!

But Ruskin wrote about it, had it put in print, read the proof, and printed the stuff, so no one, no matter how charitably disposed, can arise and zealously declare that this only is genuine, and that spurious. It's all genuine—rubbish, bosh and all.

Titian painted some dreary, commonplace pictures, and he also painted others that must ever be reckoned as among the examples of sublime art that have made the world stronger in its day and generation and proud of what has been

Titian was essentially a pagan. When he painted Christian subjects he introduced a goodly flavor of the old Greek love of life. Indeed, there is a strong doubt whether the real essence of Christianity was ever known at Venice, except in rare individual cases.

It was the spirit of the sea-kings, and not the gentle, loving Christ, that inspired her artists and men of learning.

TITIAN

The sensuous glamour of the Orient steeped the walls of San Marco in their rainbow tints, and gave that careless, happy habit to all the Venetian folk. In Titian's time, as today, gay gallants knelt in the churches, and dark, dreamy eyes peeked out from behind mantillas, and the fan spoke a language which all lovers knew. Outside was the strong smell of the sea, and never could a sash be flung open to the azure but there would come floating in on the breeze the gentle tinkle of a guitar.

But Titian, too, as well as Giorgione, infused into his work at times the very breath of life. At the Belle d' Arte at Venice is that grand picture, " The Assumption," which for more than two hundred years was in the Church of Santa Maria de' Frari. When Napoleon appointed a commission to select the paintings in Venice that were considered best worth preserving and protecting, and take them to the Belle d' Arte, this picture was included in the list. It was then removed from its place, where it had so long hung, above the grave of the man who executed it.

I have several large photographs of this picture, showing different portions of it. One of these pictures reveals simply the form of the Virgin. She rises from the earth, caught up in the clouds, the drapery streaming in soft folds, and on the upturned face is a look of love and tenderness and trust, combined with womanly strength, that hushes us into tears.

TITIAN

Surely there is an upward law of gravitation as well as a gravitation that pulls things down. Titian has shown us this. And as he drew over and over again in his pictures the forms and faces of the men and women he knew, so I imagine that this woman was a woman he knew and loved. She is not a far-off, tenuous creature, born of dreams: she is a woman who has lived, suffered, felt, mayhap erred, and now turns to a Power, not herself, eternal in the heavens. Into this picture the artist infused his own exalted spirit, for the mood we behold manifest in others is usually but the reflection of our own spirit.

In some far-off eon, ere this earth-journey began, some woman looked at me that way once, just as Titian has this woman look, with the same melting eyes and half-parted lips, and it made an impression on my soul that subsequent incarnations have not effaced.

I bought the photograph in Venice, at Ongania's, and paid three dollars for it. Then I framed it in simple, unplaned, unstained cedar, and it hangs over my desk now as I write.

When I am tired and things go wrong, and the round blocks all seem to be getting into the square holes, and remembrances of the lawyer who cheated me out of a hundred pounds come stealing like a blight over my spirit, I look up at the face of this woman who is not only angelic but human. I behold the steady upward flight and the tender look of pity, and my

TITIAN

soul reaches out, grasping the hem of the garment of Her who we are told was the Mother of God, and with Her I leave the old sordid earth far beneath and go on, and on, and up, and up, and up, until my soaring spirit mingles and communes with the great Infinite.

ANTHONY VAN DYCK

ANTHONY VAN DYCK

His pieces so with live objects strive,
That both or pictures seem, or both alive.
Nature herself, amaz'd, does doubting stand,
Which is her own and which the painter's hand,
And does attempt the like with less success,
When her own work in twins she would express.
His all-resembling pencil did outpass
The magic imagery of looking-glass.
Nor was his life less perfect than his art.
Nor was his hand less erring than his heart.
There was no false or fading color there,
The figures sweet and well-proportioned were.
—*Cowley's " Elegy on Sir Anthony Van Dyck "*

ANTHONY VAN DYCK

THE most common name in Holland is Van Dyck. Its simple inference is that the man lives on the dyke, or near it. In the good old days when villagers never wandered far from home, the appellation was sufficient, and even now, at this late day, it is not especially inconsistent.
In Holland you are quite safe in addressing any man you meet as Van Dyck.
The ancient Brotherhood of Saint Luke, of Antwerp, was always an exclusive affair, but during the years between Fifteen Hundred Ninety-seven and Sixteen Hundred Twenty-three there were twenty-seven artists by the name of Van Dyck upon its membership register. Out of these two dozen and three names, but one interests us.
Anthony Van Dyck was the son of a rich merchant. He was born in the year Fifteen Hundred Ninety-nine— just twenty-two years after the birth of Rubens. Before Anthony was ten years old the name and fame of Rubens illumined all Antwerp, and made it a place of pilgrimage for the faithful lovers of art of Northern Europe ✺ ✺
The success of Rubens fired the ambition of young Van Dyck. His parents fostered his desires, and after he

173

ANTHONY VAN DYCK

had served an apprenticeship with the artist Van Balen, a place was secured for him in the Rubens studio. For a full year the ambitious Rubens took small notice of the Van Dyck lad, and possibly would not have selected him then as a favorite pupil but for an accident.

Rubens reduced his work to a system. While in his studio he was the incarnation of fire and energy. But at four o'clock each day he dismissed his pupils, locked the doors, and mounting his horse, rode off into the country, five miles and back.

One afternoon, when the master had gone for his usual ride, several of the pupils returned to the studio, wishing to examine a certain picture, and by hook or by crook gained admittance. On an easel was a partly finished canvas, the paint fresh from the hands of the master. The boys examined the work and then began to scuffle —boys of sixteen or seventeen always scuffle when left to themselves. They scuffled so successfully that the easel was upset, and young Van Dyck fell backwards upon the wet canvas, so that the design was transferred to his trousers.

The picture was ruined.

The young men looked upon their work aghast. It meant disgrace for them all.

In despair Van Dyck righted the easel, seized a brush, and began to replace the picture ere it could fade from his memory. His partners in crime looked on with special personal interest and encouraged him with

ANTHONY VAN DYCK

words of lavish praise. He worked to within ten minutes of the time the master was due; and then all made their escape by the window through which they had entered ❧ ❧

The next day, when the class assembled, the pupils were ordered to stand up in line. Then they were catechized individually as to who had replaced the master's picture with one of his own.

All pleaded ignorance until the master reached the blond-haired Van Dyck. The boy made a clean breast of it all, save that he refused to reveal the names of his accomplices ❧ ❧

"Then you painted the picture alone?"

"Yes," came the firm answer that betokened the offender was resolved on standing the consequences ❧ The master relieved the strained tension by a laugh, and declared that he had only discovered the work was not his own by perceiving that it was a little better than he could do. Accidents are not always unlucky—this advanced young Van Dyck at once to the place of first assistant to Peter Paul Rubens.

ANTHONY VAN DYCK

COMMISSIONS were pouring in on Rubens. With him the tide was at flood. He had been down to Paris and had returned in high spirits with orders to complete that extensive set of pictures for Marie de Medici; he also had commissions from various churches; and would-be sitters for portraits waited in his parlors, quarreling about which should have first place.

Van Dyck, his trusted first lieutenant, lived in his house. The younger man had all the dash, energy and ambition of the older one. He caught the spirit of the master, and so great was his skill that he painted in a way that thoroughly deceived the patrons; they could not tell whether Rubens or Van Dyck had done the work ⚜ ⚜

This was very pleasing to Rubens. But when Van Dyck began sending out pictures on his own account, properly signed, and people said they were equal to those of Rubens, if not better, Rubens shrugged his shoulders ⚜ There was as little jealousy in the composition of Peter Paul Rubens as in any artistic man we can name; but to declare that he was incapable of jealousy, as a few of his o'er-zealous defenders did, is to apply the whitewash. The artistic temperament is essentially feminine, and jealousy is one of its inherent attributes. Of course there are all degrees of jealousy, but the woman who can sit serenely by and behold her charms ignored for those of another, by one who yesterday sat at her feet making

ANTHONY VAN DYCK

ballad to her eyebrow and sighing like a furnace, does not exist on the planet called Earth.

The artist, in any line, craves praise, and demands applause as his lawful right; and the pupil who in excellence approaches him, pays him a compliment that warms the cockles of his heart. But let a pupil once equal him and the pupil's name is anathema. I can not conceive of any man born of woman who would not detest another man who looked like him, acted like him, and did difficult things just as well. Such a one robs us of our personality, and personality is all there is of us ❧ ❧

The germ of jealousy in Rubens' nature had never been developed. He dallied with no " culture-beds," and the thought that any one could ever really equal him had never entered his mind. His conscious sense of power kept his head high above the miasma of fear.

But now a contract for certain portraits that were to come from the Rubens studio had been drawn up by the Jesuit Brothers, and in the contract was inserted a clause to the effect that Van Dyck should work on each one of the pictures.

" Pray you," said Rubens, " to which Van Dyck do you refer? There are many of the name in Antwerp."

The jealousy germ had begun to develop.

And about this time Van Dyck was busying himself as understudy, by making love to Rubens' wife. Rubens was a score of years older than his pupil, and Isabella

ANTHONY VAN DYCK

was somewhere between the two—say ten years older than Van Dyck, but that is nothing! These first fierce flames that burn in the heart of youth are very apt to be for some fair dame much older than himself. No psychologist has ever yet just fathomed the problem, and I am sure it is too deep for me—I give it up. And yet the fact remains, for how about Doctor Samuel Johnson—and did not our own Robert Louis fall desperately in love with a woman sixteen years his senior? Aye, and married her, too, first asking her husband's consent, and furtherance also being supplied by the ex-husband giving the bride away at the altar. At least, we have been told so.

Were this sketch a catalog, a dozen notable instances could be given in which very young men have been struck hard by women old enough to have nursed them as babes ✄ ✄

Van Dyck loved Isabella Rubens ardently. He grew restless, feverish, lost appetite and sighed at her with lack-luster eye across the dinner-table. Rubens knew of it all, and smiled a grim, sickly smile.

" I, too, love every woman who sits to me for a portrait. He'll get over it," said the master. " It all began when I allowed him to paint her picture."

Busy men of forty, with ambitions, are not troubled by Anthony Hope's interrogation. They glibly answer, " No, no, love is not all—it's only a small part of life—simply incidental!"

ANTHONY VAN DYCK

But Van Dyck continued to sigh, and all of his spare time was taken up in painting pictures of the matronly Isabella. He managed to work even in spite of loss of appetite; and sitters sometimes called at the studio and asked for "Master Van Dyck," whereas before there was only one master in the whole domain.

Rubens grew aweary.

He was too generous to think of crushing Van Dyck, and too wise to attempt it. To cast him out and recognize him openly as a rival would be to acknowledge his power. A man with less sense would have kicked the lovesick swain into the street. Rubens was a true diplomat. He decided to get rid of Van Dyck and do it in a way that would cause no scandal, and at the same time be for the good of the young man.

He took Van Dyck into his private office and counseled with him calmly, explaining to him how hopeless must be his love for Isabella. He further succeeded in convincing the youth that a few years in Italy would add the capsheaf to his talent. Without Italy he could not hope to win all; with Italy all doors would open at his touch ≲ ≲

Then he led him to his stable and presented him with his best saddle-horse, and urged immediate departure for a wider field and pastures new.

A few days later the handsome Van Dyck—with a goodly purse of gold, passports complete, and saddle-bags well filled with various letters of introduction to

ANTHONY VAN DYCK

Rubens' Italian friends—followed by a cart filled with his belongings, started gaily away, bound for the land where art had its birth.

" With Italy—with Italy I can win all! " he kept repeating to himself as he turned his horse's head to the South.

ANTHONY VAN DYCK

HE first day's ride took the artistic traveler to the little village of Saventhem, five miles from Brussels. Here he turned aside long enough to say good-by to a fair young lady, Anna Van Ophem by name, whom he had met a few months before at Antwerp.

He rode across the broad pasture, entered the long lane lined with poplars, and followed on to the spacious old stone mansion in the grove of trees.

Anna herself saw him coming and came out to meet him. They had not been so very well acquainted, but the warmth of a greeting all depends upon where it takes place. It was lonely for the beautiful girl there in the country: she welcomed the handsome young painter-man as though he were a long-lost brother, and proudly introduced him to her parents.

Instead of a mere call he was urged to put up his horse and remain overnight; and a servant was sent out to find the man who drove the cart with the painter's belongings, and make him comfortable.

The painter decided that he would remain overnight and make an early start on the morrow.

And it was so agreed.

There was music in the evening, and pleasant converse until a late hour, for the guest must sit up and see the moon rise across the meadow—it would make such a charming subject for a picture!

So they sat up to see the moon rise across the meadow.

ANTHONY VAN DYCK

¶ At breakfast the next morning there was a little banter on the subject of painting. Could not the distinguished painter remain over one day and give his hosts a taste of his quality?
" I surely will if the fair Anna will sit for her portrait! " he courteously replied.
The fair Anna consented.
The servant who drove the cart had gotten on good terms with the servants of the household, and was being initiated into the mysteries of making Dutch cheese.
¶ Meanwhile the master had improvised a studio and was painting the portrait of the charming Anna.
After working two whole days he destroyed the canvas because the picture was not keyed right, and started afresh. The picture was fairish good, but his desire now was to paint the beautiful Anna as the Madonna.
Van Dyck's affections having been ruthlessly uprooted but a few days before, the tendrils very naturally clung to the first object that presented itself—and this of course was the intelligent and patient sitter, aged nineteen last June.
If Rubens could not paint the picture of a lady without falling in love with her, what should be expected of his best pupil, Van Dyck?
Pygmalion loved into life the cold marble which his hand had shaped, and thus did Van Dyck love his pictures into being. All portrait-painters are sociable—they have to be in order to get acquainted with the

ANTHONY VAN DYCK

subject. The best portrait-painter in America talks like a windmill as he works, and tries a whole set round of little jokes, and dry asides and trite aphorisms on the sitter, meanwhile cautiously noting the effect. For of course so long as a sitter is coldly self-conscious, and fully mindful that he is " being took," his countenance is as stiff, awkward, and constrained as that of a farmer at a dinner-party. Hence the task devolves upon the portrait-artist to bring out, by the magic of his presence, the nature of the subject. " In order to paint a truly correct likeness, you must know your sitter thoroughly," said Van Dyck.

The gracious Rubens prided himself on his ability in this line. He would often spend half an hour busily mending a brush or mixing paints, talking the while, but only waiting for the icy mood of the sitter to thaw. Then he would arrange the raiment of his patron, sometimes redress the hair, especially of his lady patrons, and once we know he kissed the cheek of the Duchess of Mantua, "so as to dispel her distant look."

I know a portrait-artist in Albany who is said to occasionally salute his lady customers by the same token, and if they protest he simply explains to them that it was all in the interest of art—in other words, artifice for art's sake.

After three days at the charming old country-seat at Saventhem, Van Dyck called his servant and told him to take the shoes off of the saddle-horse, and turn it and

ANTHONY VAN DYCK

the cart-horse loose in the pasture. He had decided to remain and paint a picture for the village church.

And it was so done.

The pictures that Van Dyck then painted are there now in the same old ivy-grown, moss-covered church at Saventhem. The next time you are in Brussels it will pay you to walk out and see them.

One of the pictures is called " Saint Martin Dividing His Cloak With Two Beggars." The Saint is modestly represented by Van Dyck himself, seated astride the beautiful horse that Rubens gave him.

The other picture is " The Holy Family," in which the fair Anna posed for the Virgin, and her parents and kinsmen are grouped around her as the Magi and attendants ✣ ✣

Both pictures reveal the true Van Dyck touch, and are highly prized by the people of the village and the good priests of the church. Each night a priest carries in a cot and sleeps in the chancel to see that these priceless works of art are protected from harm. When you go there to see them, give the cowled attendant a franc and he will unfold the tale, not just as I have written it, but substantially. He will tell you that Van Dyck stopped here on his way to Italy and painted these pictures as a pious offering to God, and what boots it after all!

More than once have the village peasants collected, armed with scythes, hoes and pitchforks, to protect

ANTHONY VAN DYCK

these sacred pictures from vandalism on the part of lustful collectors or marauding bands of soldiers.

In Eighteen Hundred Fourteen, a detachment of French soldiers killed a dozen of the villagers, and a priest fell fighting for these treasures on the sacred threshold, stabbed to his death. Then the vandals tramped over the dead bodies, entered the church, and cut from its frame Van Dyck's "Holy Family" and carried the picture off to Paris. But after Napoleon had gotten his Waterloo (only an hour's horseback ride from Saventhem), the picture was restored to the villagers on order of the Convention.

Rubens waited expectantly, thinking to have news from his brilliant pupil in Italy. He waited a month. Two months passed, and still no word. After three months a citizen reported that the day before he had seen Van Dyck, aided by a young woman, putting up a picture in the village church at Saventhem.

Rubens saddled his horse and rode down there. He found Van Dyck and his lady-love sitting hand in hand on a mossy bank, in a leafy grove, listening to the song of a titmouse. Rubens did not chide the young man; he merely took him one side and told him that he had stayed long enough, and " beyond the Alps lies Italy." He also suggested that Anthony Van Dyck could not afford to follow the example of his illustrious Roman namesake who went down into Egypt and found things there so softly luxurious that he forgot home, friends,

ANTHONY VAN DYCK

country—all! To remain at Saventhem would be death to his art—he must have before him the example of the masters.

Van Dyck said he would think about it; and Rubens took a look at his old saddle-horse rolling in the pasture or wading knee-deep in clover, and rode back home.

In a few days he sent Chevalier Nanni down to the country-seat at Saventhem, to tell Van Dyck that he was on his way to Italy and that Van Dyck had better accompany him.

Van Dyck concluded to go. He made tearful promises to his beautiful Anna that he would return for her in a year ❧ ❧

And so the servant, who had become an expert in the making of Dutch cheese, caught the horses out of the pasture, and having rebroken them, the cavalcade started southward in good sooth.

ANTHONY VAN DYCK

IT was four years before Van Dyck returned. He visited Milan, Florence, Verona, Mantua, Venice and Rome, and made himself familiar with the works of the masters. Everywhere he was showered with attention, and the fact that he was the friend and protege of Rubens won him admittance into the palaces of the nobles.

The four years in Italy widened his outlook and transformed him from a merely handsome youth into a man of dignity and poise.

Great was his relief when he returned to Antwerp to hear that the pretty Anna Van Ophem of Saventhem had been married three years before to a worthy wine merchant of Brussels, and was now the proud mother of two handsome boys.

Great was the welcome that Van Dyck received at Antwerp; and in it all the gracious Rubens joined. But there was one face the returned traveler missed: Isabella had died the year before.

The mere fact that a man has been away for several years studying his profession gives him a decided prestige when he returns. Van Dyck, fresh from Italy, exuberant with life and energy, became at once the vogue ✣ ✣

He opened a studio, following the same lines that Rubens had, and several churches gave him orders for extensive altarpieces.

Antwerp prided herself on being an artistic center.

ANTHONY VAN DYCK

Buyers from England now and then appeared, and several of Rubens' pictures had been taken to London to decorate the houses and halls of royalty.

Portrait-painting is the first form of art that appeals to a rude and uncultivated people. To reproduce the image of a living man in stone, or to show a likeness of his face in paint, is calculated to give a thrill even to a savage. There is something mysterious in the art, and the desire to catch the shadow ere the substance fades is strong in the human heart. One reason that sacred art was so well encouraged in the Middle Ages was because the faces portrayed were reproductions of living men and women. This lent an intense personal interest in the work, and insured its fostering care. Callous indeed was the noble who would not pay good coin to have himself shown as Saint Paul, or his enemy as Judas. In fact, "Judas Receiving the Thirty Pieces of Silver" was a very common subject, and the "Judas" shown was usually some politician who had given offense ⚜ ⚜

In Sixteen Hundred Twenty-eight, England had not yet developed an art-school of her own. All her art was an importation, for although some fine pictures had been produced in England, they were all the work of foreigners—men who had been brought over from the Continent ⚜ ⚜

Henry the Eighth had offered Raphael a princely sum if he would come to London and work for a single year.

ANTHONY VAN DYCK

Raphael, however, could not be spared from Italy to do work for " the barbarians," and so he sent his pupil, Luca Penni. Bluff old Hans Holbein also abode in England and drew a goodly pension from the State.
During the reign of Mary and her Spanish husband, Philip, several pictures by Titian arrived in London, via Madrid. Then, too, there were various copies of pictures by Paul Veronese, Murillo and Velasquez that long passed for original, because the copyist had faithfully placed the great artist's trademark in the proper place ✄ ✄
Queen Elizabeth held averages good by encouraging neither art nor matrimony—whereas her father had set her the example of being a liberal patron of both. If Elizabeth never discovered Shakespeare, how could she be expected to know Raphael?
About Sixteen Hundred Twenty, the year the " Mayflower " sailed, Paul Vensomer, Cornelis Jannsen and Daniel Mytens went over to England from the Netherlands and quickly made fortunes by painting portraits for the nobility. This was the first of that peculiar rage for having a hall filled with ancestors. The artists just named painted pictures of people long gone hence, simply from verbal descriptions, and warranted the likeness to give satisfaction.
Oh, the Dutch are a thrifty folk!
James the First had no special eye for beauty—no more than Elizabeth had—but a few of his nobles were

ANTHONY VAN DYCK

intent on providing posterity with handsome ancestors, and so the portrait-painter flourished.

An important move in the cause of literature was made by King James when he placed Sir Walter Raleigh in the Tower; for Raleigh's best contributions to letters were made during those thirteen years when he was alone, with the world locked out. And when his mind began to lose its flash, the King wisely put a quietus on all danger of an impaired output by cutting off the author's head.

Still, there was no general public interest in art until the generous Charles appeared upon the scene. Charles was an elegant scholar and prided himself on being able to turn a sonnet or paint a picture; and the only reason, he explained, why he did not devote all his time to literature and art was because the State must be preserved. He could hire men to paint, but where could one be found who could govern?

Charles had purchased several of Rubens' pieces, and these had attracted much attention in London. Receptions were given where crowds surged and clamored and fought, just to get a look at the marvelous painting of the wonderful Fleming. Such gorgeous skill in color had never before been seen in England.

Charles knighted Rubens and did his best to make him a permanent attache of his Court; but Rubens had too many interests of a financial and political nature at home to allow himself to be drawn away from his beloved

ANTHONY VAN DYCK

Antwerp. ¶ But now he had a rival—the only real rival he had ever known. Van Dyck was making head. The rival was younger, handsomer, and had such a blandishing tongue and silken manner that the crowd began to call his name and declare he was greater than Cæsar.
¶ Yet Rubens showed not a sign of displeasure on his fine face—he bowed and smiled and agreed with the garrulous critics when they smote the table and declared that all of Van Dyck's Madonnas really winked.
¶ He bided his time.
And it soon came, for the agent of Lord Arundel, that great Mæcenas of the polite arts, came over to Flanders to secure treasures, and of course called on Rubens.
And Rubens talked only of Van Dyck—the marvelous Van Dyck.
The agent secured several copies of Van Dyck's work, and went back to England, telling of all that Rubens had told him, with a little additional coloring washed in by his own warm imagination.
To discover a genius is next to being one yourself. Lord Arundel felt that all he had heard of Van Dyck must be true, and when he went to the King and told him of the prodigy he had found, the King's zeal was warm as that of the agent, for does not the " messianic instinct " always live?
This man must be secured at any cost. They had failed to secure Rubens, but the younger man had no family ties, no special property interests, neither was he

ANTHONY VAN DYCK

pledged to his home government as was Rubens ⚜ ⚜ Straightway the King of England dispatched a messenger urging Anthony Van Dyck to come over to England. The promised rewards and honors were too great for the proud and ambitious painter to refuse. He started for England.

ANTHONY VAN DYCK

IN stature Van Dyck was short, but of a very compact build. He carried the crown of his head high, his chin in, and his chest out. His name is another added to that list of big-little men who had personality plus, and whose presence filled a room. Cæsar, Napoleon, Lord Macaulay, Aaron Burr and that other little man with whom Burr's name is inseparably linked, belong to the same type. These little men with such dynamic force that they can do the thinking for a race are those who have swerved the old world out of her ruts—whether for good or ill is not the question here.

When you find one of these big-little men, if he does not stalk through society a conquering Don Juan it is because we still live in an age of miracles.

Women fed on Van Dyck's smile, and pined when he did not deign to notice them. He was royal in all his tastes—his manner was regal, and so proud was his step that when he passed forbidden lines, sentinels and servants saluted and made way, never daring to ask him for card, passport or countersign.

He gloried in his power and worked it to its farthest limit ✄ ✄

Unlike Rembrandt, he never painted beggars; nor did he ever stoop as Titian did when he pictured his old mother as a peasant woman at market, in that gem of the Belle d' Arte at Venice; nor did he ever reveal on his canvas wrinkled, weather-worn old sailors, as did

ANTHONY VAN DYCK

Velasquez. ¶ He pictured only royalty, and managed, in all his portraits, to put a look of leisure and culture and quiet good-breeding into the face, whether it was in the original or not. In fact, he fused into every picture that he painted a goodly modicum of his own spirit. You can always tell a Van Dyck portrait; there is in the face a self-sufficiency, a something that speaks of "divine right"—not of arrogance, for arrogance and assumption reveal a truth which man is trying to hide, and that is that his position is a new acquirement. Van Dyck's people are all to the manner born.

He was thirty-three years old when he arrived in England ✄ ✄

King Charles furnished the painter a house at Blackfriars, fronting the Thames, to insure a good light, and gave him a summer residence in Kent. All his expenses were paid by the State, and as his tastes were regal the demands on the public exchequer were not small. His title was, "Principal Painter in Ordinary to the King and Queen of England."

Van Dyck had worked so long with Rubens that he knew how to use 'prentice talent. He studied by a system and turned off a prodigious number of canvases. The expert can at once tell a picture painted by Van Dyck during his career in England: it lacks the care and finish that was shown in his earlier years. Yet there is a subtle sweep and strength in it all that reveals the personality of the artist.

ANTHONY VAN DYCK

Twenty-two pictures he painted of King Charles that we can trace. These were usually sent away as presents. And it is believed that in the seven years Van Dyck lived in England he painted nearly one thousand portraits.

The courtly manner and chivalrous refinement of the Fleming made him a prime favorite of Charles. He was even more kingly than the King.

In less than three months after he arrived in England Charles publicly knighted him, and placed about his neck a chain of gold to which was attached a locket, set with diamonds, containing a picture of the King.

A record of Van Dyck's affairs of the heart would fill a book. His old habit of falling in love with every lady patron grew upon him. His reputation went abroad, and his custom of thawing the social ice by talking soft nonsense to the lady on the sitter's throne, while it repelled some allured others.

At last Charles grew nettled and said that to paint Lady Digby as " The Virgin " might be all right, and even to turn around and picture her as " Susanna at the Bath " was not necessarily out of place, but to show Margaret Lemon, Anne Carlisle and Catherine Wotton as " The Three Graces " was surely bad taste. And furthermore, when these same women were shown as " Psyche," " Diana " and the " Madonna " —just as it happened—it was really too much!

In fact, the painter must get married; and the King and

ANTHONY VAN DYCK

Queen selected for him a wife in the person of a Scottish beauty, Maria Ruthven.

Had this proposition come a few years before, the proud painter would have flouted it. But things were changed. Twinges of gout and sharp touches of sciatica backed up the King's argument that to reform were the part of wisdom. Van Dyck's manly shape was tending to embonpoint: he had evolved a double chin, the hair on his head was rather seldom, and he could no longer run upstairs three steps at a time. Yes, he would get married, live the life of a staid, respectable citizen, and paint only religious subjects. Society was nothing to him—he would give it up entirely.

And so Sir Anthony Van Dyck was married to Maria Ruthven, at Saint Paul's Cathedral, and the King gave the bride away, ceremonially and in fact.

Sir Anthony's gout grew worse, and after some months the rheumatism took an inflammatory turn. Other complications entered, which we would now call Bright's Disease—that peculiar complaint of which poor men stand in little danger.

The King offered the Royal Physician a bonus of five hundred pounds if he would cure Van Dyck: but if he had threatened to kill the doctor if the patient died, just as did the Greek friends of Byron, when the poet was ill at Rome, it would have made no difference ⚜

A year after his marriage, and on the day that Maria Ruthven gave birth to a child, Anthony Van Dyck

ANTHONY VAN DYCK

died, aged forty years. Rubens had died but a few months before.

The fair Scottish wife did not care to retain her illustrious name at the expense of loneliness, and so shortly married again. Whom she married matters little, since it would require a search-warrant to unearth even the man's name, so dead is he. But inasmuch as the brilliant Helena Fourment, second wife of Rubens, whose picture was so often painted by her artist-husband, married again, why shouldn't Madame Van Dyck follow the example? ✣ ✣

It is barely possible that Charles Lamb was right when he declared that no woman married to a genius ever believed her husband to be one. We know that the wife of Edmund Spenser became the Faerie Queene of another soon after his demise, and whenever Spenser was praised in her presence she put on a look that plainly said, " I could a tale unfold."

My own opinion is that a genius makes a very bad husband. And further, I have no faith in that specious plea, "A woman who marries a second time confers upon her first husband the highest compliment, for her action implies that she was so happy in her first love that she is more than willing to try it again."

I think the reverse is more apt to be the truth, and that the woman who has been sorely disappointed in her first marriage is anxious to try the great experiment over again, in order if possible to secure that bliss which

ANTHONY VAN DYCK

every daughter of Eve feels is her rightful due. ¶ Maria Ruthven lived to rear a goodly brood of children, and Samuel Pepys records that she used to send a sort o' creepy feeling down the backs of callers by innocently introducing her children thus: "This is my eldest daughter, whose father was Sir Anthony Van Dyck, of whom you have doubtless heard; and these others are my children by my present husband, Sergeant Nobody." Van Dyck's remains are buried in Saint Paul's Cathedral. A very fine monument, near the grave of Turner, marks the spot; but his best monument is in the examples of his work that are to be found in every great art-gallery of the world.

FORTUNY

FORTUNY

I think I knew Fortuny as well as any one did. He was surcharged with energy, animation and good-cheer; and the sunshine he worked into every canvas he attempted, was only a reflection of the sparkling, gem-like radiance of his own nature. He absorbed from earth, air, sky, the waters and men, and transmuted all dross into gold. To him all things were good.

—*Letter From Regnault*

FORTUNY

NOW, once upon a day there was a swart, stubby boy by the name of Mariano Fortuny. He was ten years old, going on 'leven, and lived with his grandfather away up and up four flights of rickety stairs in an old house at the village of Reus, in Spain. Mariano's father had died some years before—died mysteriously in a drunken fight at a fair, where he ran a Punch and Judy show. Some said the Devil had come and carried him off, just as he nightly did Mr. Punch.

Frowsy, little, shock-headed Mariano did n't feel so awfully bad when his father died, because his father used to make him turn the hand-organ all day, and half the night, and take up the collections; and the fond parent used to cuff him when there were less than ten coppers in the tambourine. They traveled around from place to place, with a big yellow dog and a little blue wagon that contained the show. They hitched their wagon to a dog. At night they would sleep in some shed back of a tavern, or under a table at a market, and Mariano would pillow his head on the yellow dog and curl up in a ball trying to keep warm.

When the father died, a tall man, who carried a sword and wore spurs, and had two rows of brass buttons

FORTUNY

down the front of his coat, took the dog and the wagon and the Punch and Judy show and sold 'em all—so as to get money to pay the funeral expenses of the dead man ❧ ❧
The tall man with the sword might have sold little Mariano, too, or thrown him in with the lot for good measure, but nobody seemed to want the boy—they all had more boys than they really needed already ❧
A fat market-woman gave the lad a cake, and another one gave him two oranges, and still another market-woman, fatter than the rest, blew her nose violently on her check apron and said it was too bad a boy like that did n't have a mother.
Mariano never had a mother—at least none that he knew of, and it really seemed as if it did n't make much difference, but now he began to cry, and, since the fat woman had suggested it, really wished he had a mother, after all.
There was an old priest standing by in the group. Mariano had not noticed him. But when the priest said, "But God is both our father and our mother, so no harm can come to us!" Mariano looked up in his face and felt better.
The priest's name was Father Gonzales; Mariano knew, because this is what the market-woman called him. The fat market-woman talked with the priest, and the priest talked with the man with the dangling sword, and then Father Gonzales took the boy by the hand and

FORTUNY

led him away, and Mariano trotted along by his side, quite content, save for a stifled wish that the big yellow dog might go too. And it is a gross error to suppose that a yellow dog is necessarily nothing but a canine whose capillary covering is highly charged with ocherish pigment ⚜ ⚜
Where they were going made no difference. " God is our father and our mother "—Father Gonzales said so—and, faith! he ought to know.
And by and by they came to the tall old tenement-house, and climbed up the stairs to where Mariano's old " grandfather " lived. Perhaps he was n't Mariano's sure-enough grandfather, but he was just as good as if he had been.

. . . .

But now it was an awfully long time ago since little Mariano and Father Gonzales had first climbed the stairs to where Grandfather Fortuny lived. The old grandfather and Mariano worked very hard, but they were quite content and happy. They had enough to eat, and each had a straw bed and warm blankets to cover him at night, and when the weather was very cold they made a fire of charcoal in a brazier and sat before it with spread-out hands, very thankful that God had given them such a good home and so many comforts.
¶ The grandfather made images out of white plaster, flowers sometimes, and curious emblems that people bought for votive offerings. Little Mariano's share in

FORTUNY

the work was to color the figures with blue and red paint, and give a lifelike tint to the fruit and bouquets that the grandfather cast from the white plaster.
Father Gonzales was their best customer, and used often to come up and watch Mariano paint an image of the Virgin, just as he ordered it. Mariano was very proud to receive Father Gonzales' approval; and when the image was complete he would sometimes get a copper extra for delivering the work to some stricken person that the priest wished especially to remember. For one of Father Gonzales' peculiarities was that although he bought lots of things he always gave them away ✼ ✼
Mariano used often to carry letters and packages for Father Gonzales.
One day the good priest came up the stairs quite out of breath. He carried a letter in his hand.
"Here, Mariano, my boy, you can run, while my poor old legs are full of rheumatism. Here, take this letter down to the Diligence Office and tell them to send it tonight, sure. It is for the Bishop at Barcelona and it must be in his hands before tomorrow. Run now, for the last post closes very soon."
Mariano took the letter, dived hatless out of the door and, sitting on the first stair, shot to the bottom like the slide to doom.
Grandfather Fortuny and the gentle old priest leaned out over the stone window-sill and laughed to see the

FORTUNY

boy scurry down the street. ¶ Then the priest went his way ✻ ✻

Grandfather Fortuny waited, looking out of the window, for the boy to come back. The boy did not come.
He waited.
Lights began to flicker in the windows across the way. A big red star came up in the West. The wind blew fresh and cool.
The old man shut down the sash, and looked at the untasted supper of brown bread and goat's milk and fresh fruit.
He took his hat from the peg and his cane from the corner and hobbled down the stairs. He went to the Diligence Office. No one there remembered seeing the boy— how can busy officials be expected to remember everything?
Grandfather Fortuny made his way to the house of Father Gonzales. The priest had been called away to attend a man sick unto death—he would not be back for an hour.
The old man waited—waited one hour—two.
Father Gonzales came, and listened calmly to the troubled tale of the old man. Then together they made their way over to the tall tenement and up the creaky stairway. ¶ There was the flicker of a candle to be seen under the door.
They entered, and there at the table sat Mariano munching silently on his midnight supper.

FORTUNY

" Where have you been? " was the surprised question of both old men, speaking as one person.

" Me? I 've been to Barcelona to give the letter to the Bishop—the last diligence had gone," said the boy with his mouth full of bread.

" To Barcelona—ten miles, and back? "

" Me? Yes."

" Did you walk? "

" No, I ran."

Father Gonzales looked at Grandfather Fortuny, and Grandfather Fortuny looked at Father Gonzales; then they both burst out laughing. Mariano placed an extra plate on the table, and the three drew up chairs.

FORTUNY

USINESS was looking up with Grandfather Fortuny and Mariano. All the images they made were quickly taken. People said they liked the way the cheeks and noses of the Apostles were colored; and when Father Gonzales brought in a sailor who had been shipwrecked, and the sailorman left ten pesetas for a plaster-of-Paris ship to be placed as a votive offering in the Chapel of Saint Dominic, their cup was full.

Mariano made the ship himself, and painted it, adding the yellow pennant of Spain to the mainmast.

This piece of work caused a quarrel between Grandfather Fortuny and Father Gonzales. The priest declared that a boy like that should n't waste his youth in the shabby, tumble-down village of Reus—he should go to Barcelona and receive instruction in art.

The grandfather cried and protested that the boy was all he had to love in the wide world; he himself was growing feeble, and without the lad's help at the business nothing could be done—starvation would be the end ✥ ✥

Besides, it would take much money to send Mariano to the Academy—it would take all their savings, and more! Do not inflate the child with foolish notions of making a fortune and winning fame! The world is cruel, men are unkind, and the strife of trying to win leads only to disappointment and vain regret at the last. Did not the artist Salvio commit suicide? Mariano had now a trade

207

FORTUNY

—who in Reus could make an image of the Virgin and color it in green, red and yellow so it would sell on sight for two pesetas?

Father Gonzales smiled and said something about images at two pesetas each as compared with the work of Murillo and Velasquez. He laughed at the old man's fears of starvation, and defied him to name a single case where any one had ever starved. And as for expenses, why, he had thought it all out: he would pay Mariano's expenses himself!

"Should we two old men, about ready to die, stand in the way of the success of that boy?" exclaimed the priest. "Why, he will be an artist yet, do you hear?—an artist!"

They compromised on the Grammar-School, with three lessons a week by a drawing-master.

Grandfather Fortuny did not starve. Mariano was a regular steam-engine for work. He made more images evenings, and better ones, than they had ever made before during the day.

Finally Father Gonzales' wishes prevailed and Mariano was sent to the Academy at Barcelona. Out of his own scanty income the old priest set aside a sum equal to eight dollars a month for Mariano; and when the grandfather's sight grew too feeble for him to work at his trade he moved over to the rectory.

For a year, Father Gonzales sent the eight dollars on the first of each month. And then there came to him a brusk

FORTUNY

notification from Claudio Lorenzale, the Director of the Academy, to the effect that certain sums had been provided by the City of Barcelona to pay the expenses of four of the most worthy pupils at the Academy, and Mariano Fortuny had been voted as one who should receive the benefit of the endowment.

Father Gonzales read the notice to Grandfather Fortuny, and then they sent out for a fowl, and a bottle and a loaf of bread two feet long; and together the two old men made merry.

The grandfather had now fully come to the belief that the lad would some day be a great artist.

We do not know much concerning the details of Mariano's life at Barcelona, save from scraps of information he now and then gave out to his friends Regnault and Lorenzo Valles, and which they in turn have given to us ✄ ✄

Yet we know he won the love of his teachers, and that Federico Madrazo picked out his work and especially recommended it.

Madrazo, I believe, is living now—at least he was a few years ago. He was born and bred an artist. His father, Joseph, had been a pupil under David, and was an artist of more than national renown. He served the Court at Madrid in various diplomatic relations, and won wealth and a noble name.

Federico Madrazo used to spend a portion of his time at the Academy of Barcelona as instructor and adviser to

FORTUNY

the Director. I do not know his official position, if he had one, but I know he afterward became the Director of the Museum of Art at Madrid.

Madrazo had two sons, who are now celebrated in the art world. One of them, Raimonde Madrazo, is well known in Paris, and, in Eighteen Hundred Ninety-three, had several pictures on exhibition at the Chicago Exposition; while another son, Rivera, is a noted sculptor and a painter of no small repute.

And so it was that Mariano Fortuny at Barcelona attracted the attention of Federico Madrazo, the artist patrician ❧ ❧

I can not find that Mariano's work at this time had any very special merit. It merely showed the patient, painstaking, conscientious workman. But the bright, strong, eager young man was the sort that every teacher must love. He knew what he was at school for, and did his best ❧ ❧

Madrazo said, " He's a manly fellow, and if he does not succeed he is now doing more—he deserves success."

So Mariano Fortuny and the great Madrazo, pupil and teacher, became firm friends.

And we know that, in Eighteen Hundred Fifty-seven, Mariano was voted the " Prize of Rome." Each year this prize was awarded to the scholar who on vote of the teachers and scholars was deemed most deserving. It meant two years of study at Rome with five hundred dollars a year for expenses. And the only obligation was

FORTUNY

that the pupil should each year send home two paintings: one an original and the other a copy of some old masterpiece.

The sum of two hundred fifty dollars was advanced to Mariano at once. He straightway sent one-half of the amount down to his grandfather, with particulars of the good news.

"What did I tell you?" said the grandfather. "It was I who first taught him to use a brush. I used to caution him about running his reds into his greens, and told him to do as I said and he would be a great artist yet."

Father Gonzales and Grandfather Fortuny went out and bought two fowls, three bottles, and a loaf of bread a yard long.

Mariano made all preparations to start for Rome. But the night before the journey was to begin, conscription officers came to his lodging and told him to consider himself under arrest—he must serve the State as a soldier.

It seems that the laws of Spain are such that any citizen can be called on to carry arms at any moment; and there are officials who do little but lie in wait for those who can pay, but have no time to fight. These officials are more intent on bleeding their countrymen than the enemy.

Mariano applied to his friend Madrazo for advice as to what to do, and Madrazo simply cut the Gordian knot by paying out of his own purse three hundred dollars

FORTUNY

to secure the release of the young artist. ¶ And so Mariano started gaily away, carrying with him the heart's love of two old men, and the admiring affection of a whole school.
The grandfather died three months afterward—went babbling down into the Valley, making prophecies to the last to the effect that Mariano Fortuny would yet win deathless fame.
And Father Gonzales lived to see these prophecies fulfilled ✖ ✖

FORTUNY

HEN, at twenty-two, Fortuny was ordered by the city of Barcelona to accompany General Prim on his Algerian expedition, it was a milepost on his highway of success ⚜
Nominally he was secretary to the General. Who it was secured his appointment he never knew; but we have reason to suppose it was Federico Madrazo.
Fortuny's two years in Rome had just expired; his Barcelona friends knew that the time had been well spent, and the opportunities improved, and a further transplantation they believed would result in an increased blossoming.
"Enter into life! Enter into life!" was the call of a prophet long ago. In barbaric Africa, Fortuny entered into life with the same fine, free, eager, receptive spirit that he had elsewhere shown. General Prim, soldier and scholar, saw that his secretary was capable of doing something more than keeping accounts, and so a substitute was hired and Fortuny was sent here and there as messenger, but in reality, so that he could see as many sides of old Moorish life as possible.
Staid old General Prim loved the young man just as Madrazo had. Fortuny was not much of a soldier, for war did not interest him, save from its picturesque side. "War is transient, but Beauty is eternal," he once said.
¶ Even the fact that the Spanish Army was now on the soil of her ancient enemy, the Moor, did not stir his patriotism ⚜ ⚜

FORTUNY

He sketched with feverish industry, fearing the war would end too soon, and he would have to go back with empty sketchbooks. The long stretches of white sands, the glaring sunshine, the paradox of riotous riches and ragged poverty, the veiled women, blinking camels, long rifles with butts inlaid with silver, swords whose hilts are set with precious stones, gray Arab horses with tails sweeping the ground, and everywhere the flutter of rags—these things bore in on his artist-nature and filled his heart.

He hastily painted in a few of his sketches and sent them as presents to his friends in Barcelona.

The very haste of the work, the meager outline and simple colors—glaring whites and limpid blues, with here and there a dash of red to indicate a scarf or sash—astonished his old teachers. Here were pictures painted in an hour that outmatched any of the carefully worked out, methodical attempts of the Academy! It was all life, life, life—palpitating life.

The sketches were shown, the men in power interviewed, and the city of Barcelona ordered Fortuny to paint one large picture to be eventually placed in the Parliament House to commemorate the victory of General Prim.

As an earnest of good faith a remittance of five hundred dollars accompanied the order.

The war was short. At the battle of Wad Ras the enemy was routed after a pitched fight where marked dash and

FORTUNY

spirit were shown on both sides. ¶ And so this was to be the scene of Fortuny's great painting. Hundreds of sketches were made, including portraits of General Prim and various officers. Fortuny set about the work as a duty to his patrons who had so generously paved the way for all the good fortune that was his. The painting was to be a world-beater; and Fortuny, young, strong, ambitious—knowing no such word as fail—went at the task ❧ ❧

Fortuny had associated with many artists at Rome and he had heard of that wonderful performance of Horace Vernet's, the " Taking of the Smalah of Abd-el-Kader." This picture of Vernet's, up to that time, was the largest picture ever held in a single frame. It is seventy-one feet long and sixteen feet high. To describe that picture of Vernet's with its thousand figures, charging cavalry, flashing sabers, dust-clouds, fleeing cattle, stampeding buffalos, riderless horses, overturned tents, and fear-stricken, beautiful women would require a book.

In passing, it is well to say that this picture of Vernet's is the parent of all the panorama pictures that have added to the ready cash of certain enterprising citizens of Chicago, and that Vernet is the father of the modern " military school."

If you have seen Vernet's painting you can never forget it, and if there were nothing else to see at Versailles but this one picture you would be repaid, and amply repaid, for going out from Paris to view it.

FORTUNY

Before beginning his great canvas Fortuny was advised to go to Versailles and see the Vernet masterpiece. He went and spent three days studying it in detail.

He turned away discouraged. To know too much of what other men have said is death to a writer; for an artist to be too familiar with the best in art is to have inspiration ooze out at every pore.

Fortuny took a week to think it over. He was not discouraged—not he—but he decided to postpone work on the masterpiece and busy himself for a while with simpler themes. He remained at Paris and made his thumb-nail sketches: a Moor in spotless white robe with red cap, leaning against a wall; a camel-driver at rest; a solitary horseman with long spear, a trellis with climbing vines, and a veiled beauty looking out from behind, etc.

And in all these pictures is dazzling sunshine and living life. The joy of them, the ease, the grace, the beauty, are matchless.

Goupil and Company, the art-dealers, contracted to take all the work he could turn out. And Fortuny did not make the mistake of doing too much. He possessed the artistic conscience, and nothing left his studio that did not satisfy his heart and head.

Trips had been taken to Florence, Venice and the beloved Morocco, and the poise and grace and limpid beauty of Fortuny's pictures seemed to increase.

Three years had passed, and now came a letter from the

FORTUNY

authorities at Barcelona asking for their great battle picture, and a remittance was sent " to meet expenses."
¶ Fortuny promised, and made an effort at the work ✣ Another year went by and another letter of importunity came. Barcelona did not comprehend how her gifted son was now being counted among the very ablest artists in Paris—that world center of art. Artists should struggle for recognition, be rebuffed, live on a crust in dingy garrets, cultivate a gaunt and haggard look, and wear suits shiny at the elbows!
How could the old professors down at Barcelona understand that this mere youth was pressed with commissions from rich Americans, and in receipt of a princely income?
¶ Fortuny returned all the money that Barcelona had sent him, regarding it all as a mere loan, and promised to complete the battle picture whenever he could bring his mind to bear upon it so that the work would satisfy himself ✣ ✣
The next year he visited Spain and was received at Madrid and Barcelona as a prince. Decorations and ceremonials greeted him at Madrid; and at Barcelona there were arches of triumph built over the streets, and a hundred students drew his carriage from the steamboat-landing up to the old Academy where he used to draw angles and curves from a copy all day long.
And it was not so many moons after this little visit to Barcelona that wedding-bells were sent a-swing, and Mariano Fortuny was married to Cecilia, daughter of

FORTUNY

Federico Madrazo. ¶ Their honeymoon of a year was spent at the Alhambra Palace amid the scenes made famous by our own Washington Irving. And it was from Granada that he sent a picture to America to be sold for the benefit of the sufferers in the Chicago fire ⚜ ⚜ But there were no idle days. The artist worked with diligence, dipping deep into the old Moorish life, and catching the queer angles of old ruins and more queer humanity upon his palette. His noble wife proved his mate in very deed, and much of his best work is traceable to her loving criticism and inspiration.

Paris, Granada and Rome were their home, each in turn. The prices Fortuny realized were even greater than Meissonier commanded. Some of his best pieces are owned in America, through the efforts of W. H. Stewart of Philadelphia. At the A. T. Stewart sale, in New York, the " Fortunys " brought higher prices than anything else in the collection, save, I believe, the " 1807 " of Meissonier. In fact, there are more " Fortunys " owned in New York than there are in either Barcelona or Madrid.

Indeed, there is a marked similarity between the style of Fortuny and that of Meissonier. When some busybody informed Meissonier that Fortuny was imitating him, Meissonier replied, " To have such a genius as Mariano Fortuny imitate me would be the greatest happiness of my whole career."

Fortuny's life is mirrored in his name: his whole career

FORTUNY

was one triumphant march to fortune, fame, love and honor ⚜ ⚜

He avoided society, as he was jealous of the fleeting hours, and his close friends were few; but those who knew him loved him to a point just this side of idolatry.
¶ Fortuny died at Rome on November Twenty-second, Eighteen Hundred Seventy-two, of brain rupture—an instant and painless death. In his short life of thirty-six years he accomplished remarkable results, but all this splendid work he regarded as merely in the line of preparation for a greater work yet to come.

For some weeks before he died he had been troubled with a slight fever, contracted, he thought, from painting in a damp church; but the day of his death he took up his brush again and, as he worked, gaily talked with his wife of their plans for the future.

It is very pleasant to recall, however, that before death claimed him, Fortuny had completed the great picture of " The Battle of Wad Ras." The canvas is now hanging on the wall of the Parliament House at Barcelona, and the picture is justly the pride of the city that showed itself such a wise and loving mother to the motherless boy, Mariano Fortuny.

FORTUNY

TALY and Spain are sisters, and not merely first cousins, as Mr. Whistler once remarked. Their history to a great degree is contemporaneous. They have seen dynasties arise, grow old, and die; and schools of art, once the pride of the people, sink into blank forgetfulness: for schools, like dynasties and men, live their day and go tottering to their rest.

Italy, as the elder sister, has set the fashion for the younger. The manners, habits and customs of the people have been the same.

To a great extent all art is controlled by fad and fashion; and all the fashions in the polite arts easily drifted from Italy into Spain. The works of Titian carried to Madrid produced a swarm of imitators, some of whom, like Velasquez, Zurbaran, Ribera and Murillo, having spun their cocoons, passed through the chrysalis stage, developed wings, and soared to high heaven. But the generations of imitators who followed these have usually done little better than gape.

And although Spain has been a kind mother to art for four hundred years, yet the modern school of Spanish art shows no " apostolic succession " from the past. It is a thing separate and alone: gorgeous, dazzling, strong, and rarely beautiful. Totally unlike the art of the old masters, it takes its scenes from Nature and actual living life—depending not on myth, legend or fable. It discards pure imagination, and by holding a mirror up

FORTUNY

to Nature has done the world the untold blessing of introducing it to itself.

The average man sees things in the mass, and therefore sees nothing; everything, to his vision, is run together in hopeless jumble: all is discord, confusion—inextricable confusion worse confounded.

But the artist who is also a scientist (whether he knows it or not) discovers that in the seeming confusion, order, method and law yet reign supreme. And to prove his point he lifts from the tangle of things one simple, single scene and shows this, and this alone, in all its full and rounded completeness—beautiful as a snow-crystal on the slide of a microscope.

All art consists in this: to show the harmony of a part. And having seen the harmony of a part we pass on to a point where we can guess the harmony of the whole. Whether you be painter, sculptor, musician or writer, all your endeavors are toward lifting from the mass of things a scene, a form, a harmony, a truth, and, relieving it from all that distracts, catch it in immortal amber ❧ ❧

The writer merely unearths truth: truth has always existed: he lifts it out of the mass, and holding it up where others can see it, the discerning cry, "Yes, yes—we recognize it!" The musician takes the sound he needs from the winds blowing through the forest branches, constructs a harp strung with Apollo's golden hair, and behold, we have a symphony! The wrongs of a

FORTUNY

race in bondage never touched the hearts of men until a woman lifted out a single, solitary black man and showed us the stripes upon the quivering back of Uncle Tom. One human being nailed to a cross reveals the concentrated woes of earth; and as we gaze upon the picture, into our hard hearts there comes creeping a desire to lessen the sorrows of the world by an increased love; and a gentleness and sympathy are ours such as we have never before known.

Fortuny is king of the modern school of Spanish painters. His genius made an epoch, and worked a revolution in the art of his country—and, some have said, in the art of the time.

As a nation it may be that Spain is crumbling into dust, but her rotting ruins will yet fertilize many a bank of violets. Certain it is that no modern art surpasses the art of Spain; and for once Italy must go to Spain for her pattern.

ARY SCHEFFER

ARY SCHEFFER

The artistic tastes of the Princess, the lofty range of her understanding, her liberality, and the sterling benevolence of her mind all combined to engender a coldness and lack of sympathy between herself and the persons composing the Court.
In the heart of the Princess dwelt a deep religious faith, such as becomes a noble, womanly heart. Nevertheless, her ardent mind sought to penetrate every mystery, so she was often accused of being a doubter—when the reverse was really true.
—*Ary Scheffer to His Brother Arnola*

ARY SCHEFFER

THE artistic evolution of Ary Scheffer was brought about mainly through the influence of three women. In the love of these women he was bathed, nourished and refreshed; their approbation gave direction to his efforts; for them he lived and worked; while a fourth woman, by her inability to comprehend the necessities of such a genius, clipped his wings, so that he fell to earth and his feet mired in the clay ⚜ ⚜

The first factor in the evolution of Scheffer, in point of both time and importance, was his mother. She was the flint upon which he tried his steel: his teacher, adviser, critic, friend. She was a singularly strong and capable woman, seemingly slight and fragile, but with a deal of whipcord, sinewy strength in both her physical and mental fiber.

No one can study the lives of eminent artists without being impressed with the fact that the artist is essentially the child of his mother. The sympathy demanded to hold a clear, mental conception—the imagination that sees the whole, even when the first straight line is made —is the gift of mother to son. She gives him of her spirit, and he is heir to her love of color, her desire for harmony and her hunger for sympathy. These, plus his

ARY SCHEFFER

masculine strength, may allow him to accomplish that which was to her only a dream.

If a mother is satisfied with her surroundings, happy in her environment, and therefore without "a noble discontent," her children will probably be quite willing to have a good time on the "unearned increment" that is their material portion. Her virtue and passive excellence die with her, and she leaves a brood of mediocrities ⚜

Were this miraculous scheme of adjustment lacking in the Eternal Plan, wealth, achievement and talent could be passed along in a direct line and the good things of earth be corraled by a single family.

But Nature knows no law of entail; she does, however, have her Law of Compensation, and this is the law which holds in order the balance of things. If a man accumulates a vast fortune, he probably also breeds spendthrifts who speedily distribute his riches; if he has great talent, the talent dies with him, for he only inspires those who are not of his blood; and if a woman is deprived of the environment for which her soul yearns, quite often her children adjust the average by working out an answer to her prayer.

When twenty-eight years of age we find Madame Scheffer a widow, with three sons: by name, Ariel, Henri and Arnold.

Madame Scheffer had a little money—not much, but enough to afford her a small, living income.

She might have married again, or she could have kept

ARY SCHEFFER

her little " dot " intact and added interest to principal by going and living with kinsmen who were quite willing to care for her and adopt her children.

But no; she decided to leave the sleepy little Dutch village where they lived in Holland, and go down to Paris ✣ ✣

And so she thrust her frail bark boldly out upon the tide, hoping and expecting that somewhere and sometime the Friendly Islands would be reached. She would spend her last sou in educating her boys, and she knew, she said, that when that was gone, God would give them the power and inclination to care for her and provide for themselves. In short, she tumbled her whole basket of bread upon the waters, fully confident that it would come back buttered. Her object in moving to Paris was that her boys could acquire French, the language of learning, and also that they might be taught art ✣ ✣

And so they moved to the great, strange world of Paris—Paris the gay, Paris the magnificent, Paris that laughs and leers and sees men and women go down to death, and still laughs on.

They lived, away up and up in a tenement-house, in two little rooms. There was no servant, and the boys took hold cheerfully to do the housekeeping, for the mother was n't so very strong.

The first thing was to acquire the French language, and if you live in Paris the task is easy. You just have to—

ARY SCHEFFER

that's all. ¶ Madame Scheffer was an artist of some little local repute in the village where they had lived, and she taught her boys the rudiments of drawing.

Ariel was always called Ary. When he grew to manhood he adopted this pet name his mother had playfully given him. He used to call her "Little Mother." Shortly after reaching Paris, Ary was placed in the studio of M. Guerin. Arnold showed a liking for the Oriental languages, and was therefore allowed to follow the bent of his mind. Henry waxed fat on the crumbs of learning that Ary brought home.

And so they lived and worked and studied; very happy, with only now and then twinges of fear for the future, for it would look a little black at times, do all they could to laugh away the clouds. It was a little democracy of four, with high hopes and lofty ideals. Mutual tasks and mutual hardships bound them together in a love that was as strong as it was tender and sweet.

Two years of Paris life had gone by, and the little fund that had not been augmented by a single franc in way of income had dwindled sadly.

In six months it was gone.

They were penniless.

The mother sold her wedding-ring and the brooch her husband had given her before they were married.

Then the furniture went to the pawnbroker's, piece by piece ✄ ✄

One day Ary came bounding up the stairs, three steps

ARY SCHEFFER

at a time. He burst into the room and tossed into his mother's lap fifty francs.

When he got his breath he explained that he had sold his first picture.

Ary, the elder boy, was eighteen; Henri, the younger, was thirteen. "It was just like a play, you see," said Ary Scheffer, long years afterward. "When things get desperate enough they have to mend—they must. The pictures I painted were pretty bad, but I really believe they were equal to many that commanded large prices, and I succeeded in bringing a few buyers around to my views. Genius may starve in a garret, if alone; but the genius that would let its best friends starve, too, being too modest to press its claims, is a little lacking somewhere." ❧ ❧

Young Scheffer worked away at any subject he thought would sell. He painted just as his teacher, Guerin, told him, and Guerin painted just like his idol, David, or as nearly as he could.

Art had gotten into a fixed groove; laws had been laid down as to what was classic and what not. Conservatism was at the helm.

Art, literature, philosophy, science, even religion, have their periods of infancy, youth, manhood and decay. And there comes a time to every school, and every sect, when it ceases to progress. When it says, "There now, this is perfection, and he who seeks to improve on it is anathema," it is dead, and should be buried. But schools

ARY SCHEFFER

and sects and creeds die hard. Creeds never can be changed: they simply become obsolete and are forgotten; they turn to dust and are blown away on the free winds of heaven.

The art of the great David had passed into the hands of imitators. It had become a thing of metes and bounds and measurements and geometric theorems. Its colors were made by mixing this with that according to certain fixed formulas.

About this time a young playwright by the name of Victor Hugo was making much din, and the classics as a consequence were making mighty dole and endeavoring to hiss him down. The Censor had forbidden a certain drama of Hugo's to be played until it had been cut and trimmed and filed and polished, and made just like all other plays.

Victor Hugo was the acknowledged leader of the spirit of protest; in lyric music Rossini led; and Delacroix raised the standard of revolt in painting. With this new school, which called itself "Romanticism," Madame Scheffer and her sons sincerely sympathized. The term "Romanticism" of itself means little, or nothing, or everything, but the thing itself is the eternal plea for the right of the individual—a cry for the privilege to live your own life and express the truth as you feel it, all in your own way. It is a revolution that has come a thousand times, and must and will come again and again. When custom gets greater than man it must be

ARY SCHEFFER

broken. The ankylosis of artistic smugness is no new thing. In heart and taste and ambition Ary and the Little Mother were one. Madame Scheffer rejoiced in the revolt she saw in the air against the old and outgrown. She was a Republican in all her opinions and ideals; and these feelings she shared with her boys. They discussed politics and art and religion over the teacups; and this brave and gentle woman kept intellectual pace with her sons, who in merry frolic often carried her about in their arms. Only yesterday, it seemed to her, she had carried them, and felt upon her face the soft caress of baby hands. And now one of these sons stood a foot higher than she.

Ary Scheffer was tall, slender, with a thoughtful, handsome face. The habit of close study, and the early realization of responsibilities had hastened his maturity. Necessity had sharpened his business sense and given a practical side to his nature, so he deferred enough to the old world to secure from it the living that is every man's due ⁂ ⁂

His pictures sold—sold for all they were worth. The prices were not large, but there was enough money so that the gaunt wolf that once scratched and sniffed at the door was no longer to be seen nor heard.

They had all they needed. The Little Mother was the banker, and we may safely guess that nothing was wasted ⁂ ⁂

Pupils now came to Ary Scheffer—dull fellows from the

ARY SCHEFFER

schools, who wished to be coached. Sitters in search of good portraits, cheap for cash, occasionally climbed the stairway. The Little Mother dusted about and fixed up the studio so as to make it look prosperous.

One fine lady came in a carriage to sit for her portrait. She gave her wraps into the keeping of the Little Mother at the door, with an admonitory, " Take care of these, mind you, or I 'll report you to your master."

The Little Mother bowed low and promised.

That night when she told at the supper-table how the fine lady had mistaken her for a servant, Henri said, " Well, just charge the fine lady fifty francs extra in the bill for that."

But Ary would not consent to let the blunder go so cheaply. When the fine lady came for her next sitting, the Little Mother was called and advised with at length as to pose and color-scheme.

Neither was the advising sham, for Ary deferred to his mother's judgment in many ways, and no important step was taken without her approval. They were more like lovers than mother and son. His treatment of her was more than affectionate—it was courteous and deferential, after the manner of men who had ancestors who were knights of the olden time.

The desire to sit on a divan and be waited upon is the distinguishing feature of the heartless mistress of fortune. Like the jeweled necklace and bands of gold at wrist and waist, which symbol a time when slavery was

ARY SCHEFFER

rife and these gauds had a practical meaning, so does the woman who in bringing men to her feet by beck and nod tell of animality too coarse for speech.

But the woman with the great, tender and loving heart gives her all and asks no idolatrous homage. Her delight is in serving, and willingly and more than willingly, for without thought she breaks the vase of precious ointment and wipes the feet of the beloved with the hairs of her head.

Madame Scheffer sought in all ways to serve her sons, and so we find there was always a gentle rivalry between Ary and his mother as to who could love most.

She kept his studio in order, cleaned his brushes and prepared the canvas. In the middle of the forenoon she would enter his workroom with tea and toast or other little delicacies that he liked, and putting the tray down, would kiss the forehead of the busy worker and gently tiptoe out.

When the day's work was done she intelligently criticized and encouraged; and often she would copy the picture herself and show how it could be changed for the better here or there.

And all this fine, frank, loving companionship so filled Ary's heart that he put far behind him all thought of a love for another with its closer tie. He lived and worked for the Little Mother. They were very happy, for they were succeeding. They had met the great, cruel world, the world of Paris that romps and dances and laughs,

ARY SCHEFFER

and sees struggling and sad-eyed women and men go down to their death, and still laughs on; they had met the world in fair fight and they had won.

The Little Mother had given all for Ary; on his genius and ability she had staked her fortune and her life. And now, although he was not twenty-one, she saw all that she had given in perfect faith, coming back with interest ten times compounded.

The art world of Paris had both recognized and acknowledged the genius of her boy—with that she was content.

ARY SCHEFFER

N the year Eighteen Hundred Eighteen, we find General Lafayette writing to Lady Morgan in reference to a proposed visit to the Chateau de la Grange. He says: " I do not think you will find it dull here. Among others of our household is a talented young painter by the name of Scheffer." ⚜ ⚜

Later, Lady Morgan writes to friends in England from La Grange, "Ary Scheffer, a talented artist, is a member of our company here at the chateau. He is quite young, but is already a person of note. He is making a portrait of the General, and giving lessons to the young ladies in drawing, and I, too, am availing myself of his tutorship." ⚜ ⚜

Through his strong Republican tendencies Scheffer had very naturally drifted into the company of those who knew Lafayette. The artist knew the history of the great man and was familiar with his American career. Scheffer was interested in America, for the radicals with whom he associated were well aware that there might come a time when they would have to seek hastily some hospitable clime where to think was not a crime. And indeed, it is but natural that those with a penchant for heresy should locate a friendly shore, just as professional criminals study the extradition laws ⚜ Lafayette, Franklin and Washington had long been to Scheffer a trinity of familiar names, and when an opportunity came to be introduced to the great

ARY SCHEFFER

Franco-American patriot he gladly took advantage of it ⚜ ⚜

Lafayette was sixty-one; Scheffer was twenty-three, but there at once sprang up a warm friendship between them. Not long after their first meeting Scheffer was invited to come to La Grange and make it his home as long as he cared to.

The Little Mother urged the acceptance of such an invitation. To associate for a time with the aristocratic world would give the young man an insight into society and broaden his horizon.

In the family of Lafayette, Scheffer mingled on an equality with the guests. His conversation was earnest, serious and elevated; and his manner so gracious and courtly that he won the respect of all he met. Lady Morgan intimates that his simplicity of manner tempted the young ladies who were members of his class in drawing to cut various innocent capers in his presence, and indulge in sly jokes which never would have been perpetrated had the tutor been more of a man of the world.

It has happened more than once that men of the highest spirituality have had small respect for religion, as it is popularly manifested. The machinery of religion and religion itself are things that are often widely separated; and Ary Scheffer was too high-minded and noble to worship the letter and relinquish the spirit that maketh alive. He was of that type that often goes through the

ARY SCHEFFER

world scourged by a yearning for peace, and like the dove sent out from the Ark finding no place to rest. All about he beheld greed, selfishness, hypocrisy and pretense. He longed for simplicity and absolute honesty, and was met by craft and diplomacy. He asked for religion, and was given a creed.

And so into the hearts of such as he there comes creeping a spirit of revolt. Instead of accepting this topsy-turvy old world and making the best of it, their eyes are fixed upon an ideal that Heaven alone can realize ✣
The home of Lafayette was the rendezvous of the discontented. Art, literature, politics and religion were all represented in the parlors of La Grange. Where Franklin had discoursed Poor Richard philosophy, there now gathered each Sunday night a company in which " the greatest of the Americans " would have delighted. For this company, no question was too sacred for frank and free discussion.

It was at the home of Lafayette that Scheffer met Augustin Thierry, and between these two there grew a friendship that only death was to divide.

But there was one other person Scheffer met at La Grange who was to exercise a profound influence on his life: this was the Duchess of Orleans. The quiet manliness of the young artist impressed the future Queen of France, and he was invited to Neuilly to copy certain portraits ✣ ✣
In the year Eighteen Hundred Twenty-six, we find

ARY SCHEFFER

Scheffer regularly established in the household of the Duke and Duchess of Orleans, with commissions to paint portraits of all the members of the family, and incidentally to give lessons in drawing and mathematics to the Princess Marie.

The Princess had been a sore trial to her parents, in that she had failed to fit into the conventional ways of polite society. Once she had shocked all Neuilly by donning man's attire and riding horseback astride. A worthy priest who had been her tutor had found her tongue too sharp for his comfort, and had resigned his post in dismay. The Princess argued religion with the Bishop and discussed politics with visitors in such a radical way that her father often turned pale. For the diversions of society she had a profound contempt that did not fail to manifest itself in sharp sallies against the smug hypocrisy of the times. She had read widely, knew history, was familiar with the poets, and had dived into the classics to a degree equaled by few women in France. So keen was her wit that, when pompous dignitaries dined at Neuilly, her father and mother perspired freely, not knowing what was coming next. In her character were traits that surely did not belie her Louis Quatorze ancestry ⚜ ⚜

And yet this father and mother had a certain secret pride in the accomplishments of their daughter. Parents always do. Her independence sort of kept them vibrating between ecstasies of joy and chills of fear.

ARY SCHEFFER

The Princess was plain in feature but finely formed, and had attracted the favorable attention of various worthy young men, but no man had ever dared to make love to her except by post or proxy. Several lovers had pressed their claims, making appeal through her father; but the Duke of Orleans, strong as he was, never had cared to intimate to his daughter a suggestion as to whom she should wed. Love to her was a high and holy sacrament, and a marriage of convenience or diplomacy was to the mind of the Princess immoral and abhorrent.
The father knew her views and respected them.
But happiness is not a matter of intellect. And in spite of her brilliant, daring mind the Princess of Orleans was fretting her soul out against the bars of environment: she lacked employment; she longed to do, to act, to be ❧ ❧
She had ambitions in the line of art, and believed she had talent that was worth cultivating.
And so it was that Ary Scheffer, the acknowledged man of talent, was invited to Neuilly.
He came.
He was twenty-nine years of age; the Princess was twenty-five ❧ ❧
The ennui of unused powers and corroding heart-hunger had made the Princess old before her time. Scheffer's fight with adversity had long before robbed him of his youth ❧ ❧
These two eyed each other curiously.

ARY SCHEFFER

The gentle, mild-voiced artist knew his place and did not presume on terms of equality with the Princess who traced a direct pedigree to Louis the Great. He thought to wait and allow her gradually to show her quality ⚜
She tried her caustic wit upon him, and he looked at her out of mild blue eyes and made no reply. He had no intention of competing with her on her own preserve; and he had a pride in his profession that equaled her pride of birth.
He looked at her—just looked at her in silence. And this spoilt child, before whom all others quailed, turned scarlet, stammered and made apology.
In good sooth, she had played tierce and thrust with every man she had met, and had come off without a scar; but here was a man of pride and poise, and yet far beneath her in a social way, and he had rebuked her haughty spirit by a simple look.
A London lawyer has recently put in a defense for wife-beating, on the grounds that there are women who should be chastised for their own good. I do not go quite this far, but from the time Scheffer rebuked the Princess of Orleans by refusing to reply to her saucy tongue there was a perfect understanding between them. The young woman listened respectfully if he spoke, and when he painted followed his work with eager eyes.
At last she had met one who was not intent on truckling for place and pelf. His ideals were as high and excellent as her own—his mind more sincere. Life was more to

ARY SCHEFFER

him than to her, because he was working his energies up into art, and she was only allowing her powers to rust.

She followed him dumbly, devotedly.

He wished to treat her as an honored pupil and with the deference that was her due, but she insisted that they should study and work as equals.

Instead of giving the young woman lessons to learn, they studied together. Her task as pupil was to read to him two hours daily as he worked, and things she did not fully understand he explained.

The Princess made small progress as a painter, probably because her teacher was so much beyond her that she was discouraged at thought of equaling him; and feeling that in so many other ways they were equals, she lost heart in trying to follow him in this.

At length, weary of attempts at indifferent drawing, the Princess begged her tutor to suggest some occupation for her where they could start afresh and work out problems together. Scheffer suggested modeling in clay, and the subject was taken up with avidity.

The Princess developed a regular passion for the work, and group after group was done. Among other figures she attempted was an equestrian statue of Joan of Arc. ¶ This work was cast in bronze and now occupies an honored place at Versailles.

So thoroughly did the young woman enter into the spirit of sculpture that she soon surpassed Scheffer in this

ARY SCHEFFER

particular line; but to him she gave all credit. ¶ Her success was a delight to her parents, who saw with relief that the carping spirit of cynicism was gone from her mind, and instead had come a kindly graciousness that won all hearts.

In the ability to think and act with independence there was something decidedly masculine in the spirit of the Princess Marie; and, as I have shown, Scheffer possessed a sympathy and gentleness that was essentially feminine (which is quite a different thing from being effeminate). These two souls complemented each other, and their thoughts being fixed on similar ideals, how can we wonder that a very firm affection blossomed into being?

But the secret of their love has never been written, and base would be the pen that would attempt to picture it in detail.

Take off thy shoes, for the place whereon thou standest is holy ground.

The Duke and Duchess admired Scheffer, but never quite forgot that he was in their employ, and all their attempts to treat him as an equal revealed the effort. It was as though they had said: " You are lowly bred, and work with your hands, and receive a weekly wage, but these things are nothing to us. We will not think less of you, for see, do we not invite you to our board? "

The aristocracy of birth is very seldom willing to acknowledge the aristocracy of brain. And the man of

ARY SCHEFFER

brains, if lowly born, has a mild indifference, at least, for all the gilt and gaud of royalty. The Prince of Wales does not recognize the nobility of Israel Zangwill; and Israel Zangwill asks in bored indifference, " Who—who is this man you call H. R. H. ? "
But love is greater than man-made titles, and when was there ever a difference in station able to separate hearts that throbbed only for each other?
Possibly even the stern old Duke might have relented and given his blessing were it not that events of mighty importance came seething across the face of France, and duties to his country outweighed the duties to his daughter
On the Thirtieth day of July, Eighteen Hundred Thirty, Ary Scheffer was at the house of his mother in Paris. A hurried knock came at the door, and Ary answered it in person. There on the threshold stood M. Thiers.
" Oh, Scheffer! it is you, how fortunate! you are a member of the household of Orleans, and I have a most important message for the Duke. You must go with me and deliver it to him."
" I see," said Scheffer; " the Convention has named the Duke as King of France, and we are to notify him."
" Exactly so," said Thiers.
Horses were at the door: they mounted and rode away. The streets were barricaded, so carriages were out of the question, but Scheffer and Thiers leaped the barricades, and after several minor mishaps found themselves

ARY SCHEFFER

safely out of Paris. ¶ The call was not entirely unexpected on the part of the Duke. Scheffer addressed him as " Le Roi," and this told all.

The Duke hesitated, but finally decided to accept the mission, fraught with such mighty import. He started in disguise for Paris that night on foot.

At the back entrance of the Palais Royal stood Ary Scheffer, and saw Louis Philippe mingle with the crowd, unrecognized—then pass into the palace—this palace that was his birthplace.

The next day Louis appeared with Lafayette on a balcony of the Hotel de Ville, and these two embraced each other in sight of the multitude.

It is not for me to write a history of those troublous times, but suffice it to say that the " Citizen King " ruled France probably as well as any other man could have done. His task was a most difficult one, for he had to be both king and citizen—to please Royalist and Populist alike.

This sudden turn of the political kaleidoscope was a pivotal point in the life of Ary Scheffer. So long as the Duke of Orleans was a simple country gentleman, Scheffer was the intimate friend of the family, but how could the King of France admit into his family circle a mere low-born painter? Certainly not they who are descended from kings!

Orders were issued by the government to Scheffer to paint certain pictures, and vouchers reached him from

ARY SCHEFFER

official sources, but he was made to understand that friendship with the household of a king was not for him. Possibly he had been too much mixed up with the people in a political way! The favor of the populace is a thing monarchs jealously note, as mariners on a lee shore watch the wind.

The father of Louis Philippe was descended from a brother of Louis the Great, while on his mother's side he was a direct descendant of the great monarch and Madame de Montespan. Such an inbred claim to royalty was something of which to boast, but at the same time Louis Philippe was painfully sensitive as to the blot on the 'scutcheon.

The Princess Marie knew the slender tenure by which her father held his place, and although her heart was wrung by the separation from her lover, she was loyal to duty as she saw it, and made no sign that might embarrass the Citizen King.

Arnold and Henri Scheffer were each married, and working out careers. Ary and his mother lived together, loving and devoted. And into the keeping of this mother had come a grandchild—a beautiful girl-baby. They called her name Cornelie. About the mother of Cornelie the grandmother was not curious. It was enough to know that the child was the child of her son, and upon the babe she lavished all the loving tenderness of her great, welling, mother heart. She had no words but those of gentleness and love for the son that had brought

ARY SCHEFFER

this charge to her. And did she guess that this child would be the sustaining prop for her son when she, herself, was gone?

All this time the poor Princess Marie was practically a prisoner in the great palace, wearing out her heart, a slave to what she considered duty. She grew ill, and all efforts of her physicians to arouse her from her melancholy were in vain.

Her death was a severe shock to poor Scheffer. For some months friends feared for his sanity, for he would only busy his brush with scenes from Faust, or religious subjects that bordered on morbidity. Again and again he painted " Marguerite in Prison," " Marguerite Waiting," " Marguerite in Paradise " and " Mignon." Into all of his work he infused that depth of tenderness which has given the critics their cue for accusing him of " sentimentality gone mad." And in fact no one can look upon any of the works of Scheffer, done after Eighteen Hundred Thirty, without being profoundly impressed with the brooding sadness that covers all as with a garment.

From the time he met the Princess of Orleans there came a decided evolution in his art; but it was not until she had passed away that one could pick out an unsigned canvas and say positively, " This is Scheffer's! "

In all his work you see that look of soul, and in his best you behold a use of the blue background that rivals the blue of heaven. No other painter that I can recall has

ARY SCHEFFER

gotten such effects from colors so simple. ¶ But Scheffer's life was not all sadness. For even when the Little Mother had passed away, Ary Scheffer wrote calmly to his friend August Thierry: "I yet have my daughter Cornelie, and were it not for her I fear my work would be a thing of the past; but with her I still feel that God exists. My life is filled with love and light."

ARY SCHEFFER

IT was a curious circumstance that Ary Scheffer, who conducted the Citizen King to Paris, was to lead him away.
Scheffer was a Captain in the National Guard, and when the stormy times of Eighteen Hundred Forty-eight came, he put away his brushes, locked his studio, and joined his regiment.
Louis Philippe had begun as a " citizen "—one of the people—and following the usual course had developed into a monarch with a monarch's indifference to the good of the individual.
The people clamored for a republic, and agitation soon developed into revolution. On the morning of the Twenty-fourth of February, Eighteen Hundred Forty-eight, Scheffer met the son of Lafayette, who was also an officer in the National Guard.
" How curious," said Lafayette, " that we should be protecting a King for whom we have so little respect! "
¶ " Still, we will do our duty," answered Scheffer.
They made their way to the Tuileries, and posted themselves on the terrace beneath the windows of the King's private apartments. As they sat on the steps in the wan light of breaking day. Scheffer heard some one softly calling his name. He listened and the call was repeated.
¶ " Who wants me? " answered Scheffer.
" 'T is I, the Queen! " came the answer.
Scheffer looked up and at the lattice of the window saw the white face of the woman he had known so well and

ARY SCHEFFER

intimately for a full score of years. ¶ The terror of the occasion did away with all courtly etiquette.

" Who is with you? " asked the Queen.

" Only Lafayette," was the answer.

" Come in at once, both of you. The King has abdicated and you must conduct us to a place of safety."

Scheffer and his companion ran up the steps, the Queen unbolted the door with her own hands, and they entered. Inside the hallway they found Louis Philippe dressed as for a journey, with no sign of kingly trappings. With them were their sons and several grandchildren ❧ They filed out of the palace, through the garden, and into the Place de la Concorde—that spot of ghastly memories ❧ ❧

The King looked about nervously. Some of the mob recognized him.

Scheffer concluded that a bold way was the best, and stepping ahead of Louis Philippe, called in a voice of authority, " Make way—make way for the King! " ❧ The crowd parted dumb with incredulity at the strange sight.

By the fountain in the square stood a public carriage, and into this shabby vehicle of the night the royal passengers were packed.

Dumas, who had followed the procession, mounted the box ❧ ❧

Scheffer gave a quick whispered order to the driver, closed the door with a slam, lifted his hat, and the

ARY SCHEFFER

vehicle rumbled away towards the Quai. ¶ When Scheffer got back to the Tuileries the mob had broken in the iron gates at the front of the gardens, and was surging through the palace in wild disorder.
Scheffer hastened home to tell Cornelie the news of the night ⚜ ⚜

ARY SCHEFFER

HEN the Little Mother died, a daughter of Henri Scheffer came to join the household of Ary Scheffer. The name of this niece was also Cornelie.

The fact of there being two young women in the house by one name has led to confusion among the biographers. And thus it happens that at least four encyclopedias record that Ernest Renan married the daughter of Ary Scheffer. Renan married the niece, and the fact that they named their first child Ary helped, possibly, to confirm the error of the biographers.

Scheffer's life was devoted to providing for and educating these young women. He himself gave them lessons in the languages, in music, painting and sculpture. The daughter was a handsome girl; and in point of intellect kept her artist-father very busy to keep one lesson in advance. Together they painted and modeled in clay, and the happiness that came to Scheffer as he saw her powers unfold was the sweetest experience he had ever known.

The coldness between himself and the King had increased. But Louis Philippe did not forget him, for commissions came, one after another, for work to cover the walls of the palace at Versailles. With the Queen his relations were friendly—even intimate. Several times she came to his house. Her interest in Cornelie was tender and strong, and when Scheffer painted a " Mignon " and took Cornelie for a model, the Queen insisted

ARY SCHEFFER

on having the picture and paying her own price—a figure quite beyond what the artist asked.

This picture, which represents so vividly the profound pathos and depth of soul which Ary Scheffer could put upon a canvas, can now be seen in the Louvre. But the best collection of Scheffer's portraits and historical pictures is at Versailles.

In the gentle companionship of his beloved daughter, Scheffer found the meed of joy that was his due. With her he lived over the days that had gone forever, and those other days that might have been.

And when the inevitable came and this daughter loved a worthy and suitable young man, Scheffer bowed his head, and fighting hard to keep back the tears gave the pair his blessing.

The marriage of Doctor Marjolin and Cornelie Scheffer was a happy mating; and both honored the gifted father and ministered to him in every kindly way.

But so susceptible was Scheffer's nature that when his daughter had given her whole heart to another, the fine edge of his art was dulled and blunted. He painted through habit, and the work had merit, but only at rare intervals was there in it that undefinable something which all can recognize, but none analyze, that stamps the product as great art.

ARY SCHEFFER

WHEN, in the year Eighteen Hundred Fifty, Scheffer married, it was the death of his art ⚜ The artist does business on a very small margin of inspiration. Do you understand me? The man of genius is not a genius all the time. Usually he is only a very ordinary individual. There may be days or weeks that are fallow, and sometimes even years that are years of famine. He can not conquer the mood of depression that is holding him to earth ⚜ But some day the clouds suddenly clear away, the sun bursts out, and the soul of the man is alive with divine fervor. Sublime thoughts crowd upon him, great waves of emotion sweep over his soul, and as Webster said of his Hayne speech, " The air was full of reasons, and all I had to do was to reach up and seize them."

All great music and all deathless poems are written in a fever of ecstasy; all paintings that move men to tears are painted in tears.

But it is easy to break in upon the sublime mood and drag the genius back to earth. Certain country cousins who occasionally visited the family of Ralph Waldo Emerson cut all mental work off short; the philosopher laid down his pen when the cousins came a-cousining and literally took to the woods. An uncongenial caller would instantly unhorse Carlyle, and Tennyson had a hatred of all lion-hunters—not merely because they were lion-hunters, but because they broke in upon his paradise and snapped the thread of inspiration.

ARY SCHEFFER

Mrs. Grote tells us that Scheffer's wife was intelligent and devoted—in fact, she was too devoted. She would bring her sewing and watch the artist at his work. If the great man grew oblivious of her presence she gently chided him for it; she was jealous of his brothers, jealous of his daughter, even jealous of his art. She insisted not only that he should love her, but demanded that he should love nothing else. And yet all the time she was putting forth violent efforts to make him happy. As a result she put him in a mood where he loved nothing and nobody. She clipped his wings, and instead of a soaring genius we find a whimsical, commonplace man with occupation gone.

Wives demand the society of their husbands as their lawful right, and I suppose it is expecting too much to suppose that any woman, short of a saint, could fit into the bachelor ways of a dreamer of dreams, aged fifty-five ❧ ❧

Before he met the widow of General Beaudrand, Scheffer was happy, with a sweet, sad happiness in the memories of the love of his youth—the love that was lost, and being lost still lived and filled his heart.

But the society of the widow was agreeable, her conversation vivacious. He decided that this being so it might be better still to have her by him all the time. And this was what the lady desired, for it was she who did the courting.

Oliver Wendell Holmes once said, " Because I like an

ARY SCHEFFER

occasional pinch of salt is no reason why you should immerse me in brine," but Ary Scheffer, the mild, gentle and guileless, did not reason quite so far.

The vivacious Sophie took him captive, and he was shorn of his strength. And no doubt the ex-widow was as much disappointed as he; there really was no good reason why he should not paint better than ever, when here he wouldn't work at all! Lawks-a-daisy!

His spirit beat itself out against the bars, health declined, and although he occasionally made groggy efforts to shake himself back into form, his heart was not in his work.

Seven years went dragging by, and one morning there came word from London that the Duchess of Orleans, the mother of the beloved Marie, was dying. Scheffer was ill, but he braced himself for the effort, and hastily started away alone, leaving a note for Cornelie.

He arrived in England in time to attend the funeral of his lifelong friend, and then he himself was seized with a deadly illness.

His daughter was sent for, and when she came the sick man's longing desire was to get back to France. If he was to die, he wanted to die at home. "To die at home at last," is the prayer of every wanderer. Ary Scheffer's prayer was answered. He expired in the arms of his beloved daughter on June Fifteenth, Eighteen Hundred Fifty-eight, aged sixty-three years.

FRANCOIS MILLET

FRANCOIS MILLET

When I meet a laborer on the edge of a field, I stop and look at the man: born amid the grain where he will be reaped, and turning up with his plow the ground of his tomb, mixing his burning sweat with the icy rain of Autumn. The furrow he has just turned is a monument that will outlive him. I have seen the pyramids of Egypt, and the forgotten furrows of our heather: both alike bear witness to the work of man and the shortness of his days.

—Chateaubriand

FRANCOIS MILLET

EAN FRANCOIS MILLET is to art what Wagner is to music, or what Whitman is to poetry. These men, one a Frenchman, another a German, the third an American, taught the same gospel at the same time, using different languages, and each quite unaware of the existence of the others. They were all revolutionaries; and success came so tardily to them that flattery did not taint their native genius.

"Great men never come singly," says Emerson.

Richard Wagner was born in the year Eighteen Hundred Thirteen, Millet in Eighteen Hundred Fourteen, and Whitman in Eighteen Hundred Nineteen. "Tannhauser" was first produced in Eighteen Hundred Forty-five; the "Sower" was exhibited in Eighteen Hundred Fifty; and in Eighteen Hundred Fifty-five "Leaves of Grass" appeared.

The reception accorded to each masterpiece was about the same; and all would have fallen flat had it not been for the gibes and jeers and laughter which the work called forth.

Wagner was arrested for being an alleged rioter; Whitman was ejected from his clerkship and his book looked after by the Attorney-General of Massachusetts; Millet

FRANCOIS MILLET

was hooted by his fellow-students and dubbed the Wild-Man-of-the-Woods.

In a letter to Pelloquet, Millet says, " The creations that I depict must have the air of being native to their situation, so that no one looking on them shall imagine they are anything else than what they are."

In his first preface to " Leaves of Grass," Whitman writes: " The art of arts, the glory of expression and the sunshine of the light of letters is simplicity. * * * To speak in literature with the perfect rectitude and insouciance of the movement of animals and the unimpeachableness of the sentiment of trees in the woods and grass by the roadside, is the flawless triumph of art."

Wagner wrote in an Essay on Art:

" The Greek, proceeding from the bosom of Nature, attained to Art when he had made himself independent of the immediate influences of Nature.

" We, violently debarred from Nature, and proceeding from the dull ground of a Heaven-rid and juristic civilization, first reach Art when we completely turn our backs on such a civilization, and once more cast ourselves, with conscious bent, into the arms of Nature."

¶ Men high in power, deceived by the "lack of form," the innocent naivete as of childhood, the simple homeliness of expression, the absence of effort, declared again and again that Millet's work was not art, nor Wagner's "recurring theme" true music, nor Whitman's rhymeless

FRANCOIS MILLET

lines poetry. The critics refused to recognize that which was not labored: where no violence of direction was shown they saw no art. To follow close to Nature is to be considered rude by some—it indicates a lack of "culture." ✄ ✄

Millet, Wagner and Whitman lived in the open air; with towns and cities they had small sympathy; they felt themselves no better and no wiser than common folks; they associated with working men and toiling women; they had no definite ideas as to who were "bad" and who "good."

They are frank, primitive, simple. They are masculine—and in their actions you never get a trace of coyness, hesitancy, affectation or trifling coquetry. They have nothing to conceal: they look at you out of frank, open eyes. They know the pains of earth too well to dance nimbly through life and laugh the hours away. They are sober, serious, earnest, but not grim. Their faces are bronzed by sun and wind; their hands are not concealed by gloves; their shirts are open to the breast, as though they wanted room to breathe deeply and full; the boots they wear are coarse and thick-soled, as if the wearer had come from afar and yet had many long miles to go. But the two things that impress you most are: they are in no haste; and they are unafraid.

All can approach such men as these. Possibly the smug and self-satisfied do not care to; but men in distress—those who are worn, or old, or misunderstood—children,

FRANCOIS MILLET

outcasts, those far from home and who long to get back, silently slip weak hands in theirs and ask, " May we go your way ? "

Can you read " Captain, My Captain," or listen to the " Pilgrims' Chorus," or look upon " The Man With the Hoe" without tears?

And so we will continue our little journey.

FRANCOIS MILLET

CHARLES WARREN STODDARD relates that in one of the far-off islands of the South Sea, he found savages so untouched by civilization that they did not know enough to tell a lie. It was somewhat such a savage as this with whom we have to deal.

He was nineteen years old, six feet high, weighed one hundred sixty pounds, and as he had never shaved, had a downy beard all over his face. His great shock of brown hair tumbled to his shoulders. His face was bronzed, his hands big and bony, and his dark gray eyes looked out of their calm depths straight into yours—eyes that did not blink, eyes of love and patience, eyes like the eyes of an animal that does not know enough to fear ♆ ♆

He was the son of a peasant, and the descendant of a long line of peasants, who lived on the coast of Normandy—plain, toiling peasants whose lives were deeply rooted into the rocky soil that gave them scanty sustenance. If they ever journeyed it was as sailors—going out with the tide—and if they did not come back it was only because those who go down to the sea in ships sometimes never do.

And now this first-born of the peasant flock was going to leave his native village of Gruchy.

He was clad in a new suit of clothes, spun, woven, cut and sewed by the hands of his grandmother.

He was going away, and his belongings were all packed

FRANCOIS MILLET

in a sailor's canvas bag; but he was not going to sea.
¶ Great had been the preparations for this journey ※
The family was very poor: the father a day-laborer and farmer; the mother worked in the fields, and as the children grew up they too worked in the fields; and after a high tide the whole family hurried to the seashore to gather up the "varech," and carry it home for fertilizer, so that the rocky hillside might next Summer laugh a harvest ※ ※

And while the father and the mother toiled in the fields, or gathered the varech, or fished for shrimps, the old grandmother looked after the children at home. The grandmother in such homes is the real mother of the flock: the mother who bore the children has no time to manifest mother-love; it is the grandmother who nurses the stone-bruises, picks out the slivers, kisses away the sorrows, gladdens young hearts by her simple stories, and rocks in her strong, old arms the babe, as she croons and quavers a song of love and duty.

And so the old grandmother had seen "her baby" grow to a man, and with her own hands she had made his clothes, and all the savings of her years had been sewed into a belt and given to the boy.

And now he was going away.

He was going away—going because she and she alone had urged it. She had argued and pleaded, and when she won the village priest over to her side, and Father Lebrisseau in his turn had won several influential

FRANCOIS MILLET

men—why, it must be! ¶ The boy could draw: he could draw so well that he some day would be a great artist—Langlois, the drawing-master at Cherbourg, ten miles away, said so.

What if they were only poor peasants and there never had been a painter in the family! There would be now. So the priest had contributed from his own purse; and the Councilmen of Cherbourg had promised to help; and the grandmother had some silver of her own.

Jean Francois Millet was going to Paris to study to be an artist.

Tears rained down the wrinkled, leathery cheeks of the old grandmother; the mother stood by dazed and dumb, nursing a six-months-old babe; children of various ages hung to the skirts of mother and grandmother, tearful and mystified; the father leaned on the gate, smoking a pipe, displaying a stolidity he did not feel.

The diligence swung around the corner and came rattling down the single, stony, narrow street of the little village. The driver hardly deigned to stop for such common folks as these; but the grandmother waved her apron, and then, as if jealous of a service some one else might render, she seized one end of the canvas bag and helped the brown young man pass it up to the top of the diligence. Jean Francois climbed up after, carrying a little prayer-book that had been thrust into his hands—a final parting gift of the grandmother.

The driver cracked his whip and away they went

FRANCOIS MILLET

As the diligence passed the rectory, Father Lebrisseau came out and held up a crucifix; the young man took off his cap and bowed his head.

The group of watchers moved out into the roadway. They strained their eyes in the direction of the receding vehicle.

FRANCOIS MILLET

FTER a three days' ride, Jean Francois was in Paris. The early winter night was settling down, and the air was full of fog and sleet ⚜ The young man was sore from the long jolting. His bones ached, and the damp and cold had hunted out every part of his sturdy frame.

The crowds that surged through the street hurrying for home and fireside after the day's work were impatient.

¶ "Don't block the way, Johnny Crapaud!" called a girl with a shawl over her head; and with the combined shove and push of those behind, the sabot-shod young man was shouldered into the street.

There he stood dazed and bereft, with the sailor's bag on his back.

"Where do you wish to go?" asked a gendarme, not unkindly ⚜ ⚜

"Back to Gruchy," came the answer.

And the young man went into the diligence office and asked when the next stage started.

It did not go until the following morning. He would have to stay somewhere all night.

The policeman outside the door directed him to a modest tavern.

Next morning things looked a little better. The sun had come out and the air was crisp. The crowds in the street did not look quite so cold and mean.

After hunger had been satisfied, "Johnny Crapaud" concluded to stay long enough to catch a glimpse of the

FRANCOIS MILLET

Louvre, that marvel of marvels! The Louvre had been glowingly described to him by his old drawing-master at Cherbourg. Visions of the Louvre had been in his mind for weeks and months, and now his hopes were soon to be realized. In an hour perhaps he would stand and look upon a canvas painted by Rubens, the immortal Rubens! ¶ His enthusiasm grew warm.

The girl who had served him with coffee stood near and was looking at him with a sort of silent admiration, such as she might bestow upon a curious animal.

He looked up; their eyes met.

" Is it true—is it true that there are pictures by Rubens in the Louvre? " asked the young man.

The oddity of the question from such a being and the queer Normandy accent amused the girl, and she burst out laughing. She did not answer the question, but going over to a man seated at another table whispered to him. Then they both looked at the queer youth and laughed. ¶ The young countryman did not know what they were laughing at—probably they did not, either—but he flushed scarlet, and soon made his way out into the street, his luggage on his back. He wanted to go to the Louvre, but dare not ask the way—he did not care to be laughed at.

And so he wandered forth.

The shops were very marvelous, and now and again he lingered long before some window where colored prints and paintings were displayed. He wondered if the places

FRANCOIS MILLET

were artists' studios; and at one place as he looked at a series of sketches the thought came to him that he himself could do better.

This gave him courage, and stepping inside the door he set down his bag and told the astonished shopkeeper that the pictures in the window were very bad—he could paint better ones—would the proprietor not hire him to paint pictures? He would work cheap, and labor faithfully ※ ※

He was hastily hustled out into the street—to harbor lunatics was dangerous.

So he trudged on—looking for the Louvre.

Night came and the search was without reward.

Seeing a sign of "Apartments for single gentlemen," he applied and was shown a modest room that seemed within his means. The landlady was very kind; in fact, she knew people at Gruchy and had often been to Cherbourg—her uncle lived there.

Jean Francois felt relieved to find that even in busy, bustling, frivolous Paris there were friendly people; and when the kind lady suggested that pickpockets in the streets were numerous, and that he had better give his money over to her for safekeeping, he handed out his store of three hundred francs without question.

He never saw his money again.

The next day he still sought the Louvre—not caring to reveal his ignorance by asking the way.

It was several days before Fate led him along the Seine

FRANCOIS MILLET

and he found himself on the Pont Neuf. The palace stretching out before him had a familiar look. He stopped and stared. There were the palaces where history had been made. He knew the Tuileries and he knew the Louvre—he had seen pictures of both.

He walked out across the Place de la Concorde, and seeing others enter, made his way through the gates of the sacred precinct.

He was in the Palace of the Louvre; he had found the way, unaided and alone.

His deep religious nature was moved, and taking off his cap he crossed himself in a silent prayer of gratitude ❧ What his sensations were he partially pictured to his friend Sensier thirty years after: " It seemed as though I had at last attained, achieved. My feelings were too great for words, and I closed my eyes, lest I be dazzled by the sight and then dare not open them lest I should find it all a dream. And if I ever reach Paradise I know my joy will be no greater than it was that first morning when I realized that I stood within the Louvre Palace."

¶ For a week Millet visited the Louvre every day.

When the doors were unlocked each morning he was waiting on the steps; and he did not leave in the afternoon until the attendant warned him it was time to go.

¶ He lingered long before the " Raffaellos " and stood in the " Rubens Gallery " dumb with wonder and admiration ❧ ❧

There were various people copying pictures here and

FRANCOIS MILLET

there. He watched them furtively, and after seeing one young man working at an easel in a certain place for a week, he approached and talked with him.

Jean Francois told his history and the young man listened patiently. He advised that it would be foolish to go back to Gruchy at once. The youth should go to some master and show what he could do—remain and study for a little while at least; in fact, he himself would take him to Delaroche. Things looked brighter; and arrangements were made to meet on the morrow and go interview the master.

Delaroche was found and proved kindly. He examined the two sketches that Jean Francois submitted, asked a few questions, and graciously led the new applicant into the atelier, where a score of young men were sketching, and set him to work.

The letter written by Jean to the good old grandmother that night hinted at great plans for the future, and told of love, and of hope that was dauntless.

FRANCOIS MILLET

WELVE years were spent by Jean Francois in Paris—years of biting poverty and grim endurance: the sport and prey of Fate: the butt and byword of the fashionable, artistic world. ¶ Jean Francois did not belong in Paris: how can robins build nests in omnibuses?

He was at war with his environment; and the stern Puritan bias of his nature refused to conform to the free and easy ways of the gay metropolis. He sighed for a sight of the sea, and longed for the fields and homely companionship that Normandy held in store.

So we find him renouncing Paris life and going back to his own.

The grandmother greeted him as one who had won, but his father and mother, and he, himself, called it failure ⚜ ⚜

He started to work in the fields and fell fainting to the earth ⚜ ⚜

"He has been starved," said the village doctor. But when hunger had been appeased and strength came back, ambition, too, returned.

He would be an artist yet.

A commission for a group of family portraits came from a rich family at Cherbourg. Gladly he hastened thence to do the work.

While in Cherbourg he found lodgings in the household of a widow who had a daughter. The widow courted the fine young painter-man—courted him for the daughter.

FRANCOIS MILLET

The daughter married him. A strong, simple man, unversed in the sophistry of society, loves the first woman he meets, provided, of course, she shows toward him a bit of soft, feminine sympathy. This accounts for the ease with which very young men so often fall in love with middle-aged women. The woman does the courting; the man idealizes, and endows the woman with all the virtues his imagination can conjure forth. Love is a matter of propinquity.

The wife of Jean Francois was neutral salts. She desired, no doubt, to do what was right and best, but she had no insight into her husband's needs, and was incapable of guessing his latent genius.

As for the new wife's mother and kinsmen, they regarded Jean Francois as simply lazy, and thought to crowd him into useful industry. He could paint houses or wagons, and, then, did n't the shipyard folks employ painters?

¶ Well, I guess so.

Jean Francois still dreamed of art.

He longed to express himself—to picture on canvas the emotions that surged through his soul.

Disillusionment had come, and he now saw that his wife was his mate only because the Church and State said so. But his sense of duty was firm, and the thought of leaving her behind never came to him.

The portraits were painted—the money in his pocket; and to escape the importunities and jeers of his wife's relatives he decided to try Paris once more.

FRANCOIS MILLET

The wife was willing. Paris was the gateway to pleasure and ambition.
But the gaiety of Paris was not for her. On a scanty allowance of bread one can not be so very gay—and often there was no fuel.
Jean Francois copied pictures in the Louvre and hawked them among the dealers, selling for anything that was offered.
Delaroche sent for him. "Why do you no longer come to my atelier?" said the master.
"I have no money to pay tuition," was the answer.
"Never mind; I'll be honored to have you work here."
¶ So Jean Francois worked with the students of Delaroche; and a few respected his work and tried to help market his wares. But connoisseurs shook their heads, and dealers smiled at "the eccentricities of genius," and bought only conventional copies of masterpieces or studies of the nude.
Meantime the way did not open, and Paris was far from being the place the wife supposed. She would have gone back to Cherbourg, but there was no money to send her, and pride prevented her from writing the truth to her friends at home. She prayed for death, and death came. The students at Delaroche's contributed to meet the expenses of her funeral. Jean Francois still struggled on.
Delaroche and others declared his work was great, but how could they make people buy it?

FRANCOIS MILLET

A time of peculiar pinching hardship came, and Jean Francois again bade Paris adieu and made his way back to Gruchy. There he could work in the fields, gather varech on the seashore, and possibly paint portraits now and then—just for amusement.
And thus he would live out the measure of his days ✣
The visit of Jean Francois to his boyhood's home proved a repetition of the first.
Another woman married him.
Catherine Lemaire was not a brilliant woman, but she had a profound belief in her husband's genius.
Possibly she did not understand him when he talked his best, but she made a brave show of listening, and did not cross him with any little whimsical philosophies of her own ✣ ✣
She was sturdy and strong of heart; privation was nothing to her; she could endure all that Jean Francois could, and count it a joy to be with him.
She was the consoler, not he; and when the mocking indifference of the world passed the work of Jean Francois by, she said, " Who cares, so long as we know 't is good? " and measured the stocking on her nose and made merry music with the flying needles.
Soon the truth forced itself on Jean Francois and Catherine that no man is thought much of by his kinsmen and boyhood acquaintances. No one at Gruchy believed in the genius of Jean Francois—no one but the old grandmother, who daily hobbled to mass and prayed

FRANCOIS MILLET

the Blessed Virgin not to forget her boy. Jean Francois and his wife studied the matter out and talked it over at length, and they decided that to stay in Gruchy would be to forfeit all hope of winning fame and fortune.
¶ Gruchy held nothing for them; possibly Paris did ✄
And anyway, to go down in a struggle for better things was not so ignominious an end as to allow one's powers to rust out, held back only through fear of failure.
They started for Paris.
Yes, Paris remembered Jean Francois. How could Paris forget him—he was so preposterous and his work so impossible!
It was still a struggle for bread.
Marriages and births have a fixed relation to the price of corn, the sociologists say. Perhaps they are right; but not in this case.
The babies came along with the years, and all brought love with them.
The devotion of Jean Francois to his wife and children had a deep, sober, religious quality, such as we associate with Abraham and Jacob and the other patriarchs of old ✄ ✄
The heart of Millet was often wrung by the thought of the privation and hardships his wife and children had to undergo. He blamed himself for their lack of creature comforts, and the salt tears rained down his beard when he had to go home and report that he had tramped the streets all day with a picture under his arm, looking for

FRANCOIS MILLET

a buyer, but no buyer could be found. ¶ But all this time the old grandmother up in Normandy waited and watched for news from her boy.

Now and again during the years she saw his name mentioned in connection with the Salon; and once she heard a medal had been granted him, and at another time an "Honorable Mention."

Her heart throbbed in pride and she wrote congratulations, and thanked the good God for answering her prayers. Little did she know of the times when bread was cut in tiny bits and parceled out to each hungry mouth, or the days when there was no fuel and the children kept to their beds to prevent freezing.

But the few friends of Jean Francois who had forced the "Honorable Mention" and secured the medal, now got something more tangible; they induced the Government Director of Fine Arts to order from Jean Francois Millet a picture for which the artist was to receive two thousand francs; two hundred francs were paid on account and the balance was to be paid on delivery of the picture. ¶ Jean Francois hurried home with the order in his trembling fingers. Catherine read the order with misty eyes. She was not unduly elated—she knew that success must come some time. And husband and wife then and there decided that when the eighteen hundred francs were paid over to them they would move out of Paris ⚹ They would make a home in the country. People do without things in the country, but they do not starve.

FRANCOIS MILLET

You can raise vegetables, and even though the garden be small and the folks poor, God is good and the sunshine and showers come and things grow. And for fuel one can gather fagots if they are near a wood.
They would go to Barbizon—Barbizon, that tiny village on the edge of the Forest of Fontainebleau. Several artists who had been there in the Summer sketching had told them of it. The city was gradually smothering Jean Francois. He prayed for a sight of the great open stretches of pasture, and green woods and winding river ✃ ✃
And now it was all so near.
He set to work feverishly to paint the great picture that was to bring deliverance.
At last the picture was done and sent to the Director's.
¶ Days of anxious waiting followed.
The picture was accepted and paid for.
Jean Francois and Catherine cried and laughed for joy, as they tumbled their belongings into bags and bundles. The grocer who had trusted them took some of their furniture for pay, and a baker and a shoemaker compromised by accepting a picture apiece. They were going to Barbizon—going to the country—going to freedom! And so the father and the mother and the queer-looking, yellow children were perched on the top of the diligence with their bundles, bound for Barbizon. They looked into each other's faces and their joy was too great for speech.

FRANCOIS MILLET

LIVING at the village of Barbizon, or near it, were Theodore Rousseau, Hughes Martin, Louis LeRoy and Clerge.

These men were artists, and their peasant neighbors recognized them as separate and apart from themselves. They were Summer boarders. But Millet was a peasant in thought and feeling and sympathy, and mingled with the people on an absolute equality. He was peasant—and more than peasant; for the majesty of the woods, the broken rocks, the sublime stretches of meadow-lands with their sights, odors and colors intoxicated him with their beauty. He felt as if he had never before looked upon God's beautiful world.

And yet Paris was only a day's journey away! There he could find a market for his work. To be near a great city is a satisfaction to every intellectual worker, but, if he is wise, his visits to the city are far apart. All he needs is the thought that he can go if he chooses.

Millet was thirty-four years of age when he reached Barbizon. There he was to remain for the remaining twenty-seven years of his life—to live in the one house—years of toil, and not lacking in poverty, pain and anxiety, but years of freedom, for he worked as he wished and called no man master.

It is quite the custom to paint the life of Millet at Barbizon as one of misery and black unrest; but those who do this are the people who read pain into his pictures: they do not comprehend the simplicity and sublimity

FRANCOIS MILLET

and quiet joy that were possible in this man's nature, and in the nature of the people he pictured.

From the time he reached Barbizon there came into his work a largeness, a majesty and an elevation that is unique in the history of art. Millet's heart went out to humanity—the humanity that springs from the soil, lives out its day, and returns to earth. His pictures form an epic of country life, as he tells of its pains, its anxieties, its privations—yes, of its peace and abiding faith, and the joy and health and strength that comes to those who live near to Nature's heart.

Walt Whitman catalogues the workers and toilers, and lists their occupations in pages that will live; Millet shows us wood-gatherers, charcoal-burners, shepherds, gleaners, washerwomen, diggers, quarrymen, road laborers, men at the plow, and women at the loom. Then he shows the noon-hour, the moments of devotion, the joys of motherhood, the silent pride of the father, the love of brother and sister and of husband and wife. And again in the dusk of a winter night we see black-lined against the sky the bent figure of an old woman, bearing her burden of fagots; and again we are shown the plain, homely interior of a cottage where the family watches by the bedside of a dying child.

And always the picture is not quite complete—the faces are never distinct—no expression of feature is there, but the soul worked up into the canvas conveys its silent message to all those who have eyes to see and hearts

FRANCOIS MILLET

to feel. ¶ Only a love and sympathy as wide as the world could have produced the " Gleaners," the " Sower " and the " Angelus."

Millet was what he was on account of what he had endured. All art is at last autobiography.

The laborer's cottage that he took at Barbizon had but three small, low rooms. These served as studio, kitchen and bedchamber. When the family had increased to eleven, other rooms were added, and the studio was transferred to the barn, there at the end of the garden. Millet had two occupations, and two recreations, he once said. In the mornings he worked in his garden, digging, sowing, planting, reaping. In the afternoons he painted—painted until the sun got too low to afford the necessary light; then he went for his daily solitary walk through the woods and fields, coming back at dark. After supper he helped his wife with the housework, put the children to bed, and then sat and read until the clock struck midnight.

This was his simple life. Very slowly, recognition came that way. Theodore Rousseau, himself a great artist, and a man too great for jealousy, spread his fame, and the faithful Sensier in Paris lost no opportunity to aid his friend by the use of a commercial shrewdness in which Millet was woefully lacking.

Then came Corot, Daubigny, Diaz and others of giant stature, to Barbizon, and when they went back to Paris they told of Millet and his work. And then we find

FRANCOIS MILLET

Meissonier, the proud, knocking at the gate of Le Grand Rustique ❧ ❧

It is pleasant to recall that Americans were among the first to recognize the value of Millet's art. His " Sower " is the chief gem of the Vanderbilt collection; and the " Angelus " has been thought much more of in France since America so unreservedly set her seal upon it ❧ Millet died in Eighteen Hundred Seventy-five.

It was only during the last ten years of his life that he felt financially free, and even then he was far from passing rich. After his death his fame increased, and pictures he had sold for twenty dollars, soon changed hands for as many hundred.

Englishmen say that America grew Millet-mad, and it may be true that our admiration tipped a bit to t' other side; yet the fabulous prices were not always paid by Americans—the rich men of earth vied with each other for the possession of a " Millet."

The " Gleaners " was bought by the French Government for three hundred thousand francs, and is now in the Louvre " in perpetuity." This sum paid for this one picture represents a larger amount of money than passed through the hands of Millet during his entire life; and yet it is not one-half what another " Millet " brought. The " Angelus " was sold for the sum of eight hundred thousand francs—a larger amount than was ever before paid for a single canvas.

It is idle to say that no picture is worth such a sum.

FRANCOIS MILLET

Anything is worth what some one else will pay for it.
¶ The number of "Millets," it may be explained, is limited, and with men in America who have incomes of ten million dollars or more a year, no sane man dare prophesy what price the "Sower" may yet command.
¶ Millet himself, were he here, would be aghast at the prices paid for his work, and he would turn, too, with disfavor from the lavish adulation bestowed upon his name ⚜ ⚜
This homely, simple artist was a profound thinker; a sympathetic dreamer; a noble-hearted, generous man; so truthful and lovable that his virtues have been counted a weakness; and so they are—for the planet Earth ⚜ ⚜

JOSHUA REYNOLDS

JOSHUA REYNOLDS

To make it people's interest to advance you, by showing that their business will be better done by you than by any other person, is the only solid foundation of success; the rest is accident.

Reynolds to His Nephew

JOSHUA REYNOLDS

N the curious little river Plym, five miles from Plymouth, is the hamlet of Plympton. It is getting on towards two hundred years since Joshua Reynolds was born there. The place has not changed so very much with the centuries: there still stand the quaint stone houses, built on arches over the sidewalk, and there, too, is the old Norman church with its high mullioned windows. Chester shows the best example of that very early architecture, and Plympton is Chester done in pigmy.

The birthplace of Reynolds is one of these houses in the " Row "; a greengrocer now has the lower floor of the house for his shop, while his numerous family live upstairs ✣ ✣

The Reverend Samuel Reynolds also had a numerous family—there being eleven children—so the present occupation is a realistic restoration of a previous condition ✣ ✣

The grocer has a leaning toward art, for his walls are well papered with chromos and posters; and as he sold a cabbage to a good housewife he nipped off a leaf for a pen of rabbits that stood in the doorway, and talked to me glibly of Reynolds and Gainsborough. The grocer considers Gainsborough the greater artist, and surely

JOSHUA REYNOLDS

his fame is wide, like unto the hat—hated by theater-goers—that his name has rendered deathless, and which certain unkind ones declare has given him immortality. Joshua was the seventh child in the brood of five boys and six girls. The fond parents set him apart for the Church, and to that end he was placed in the Plympton Grammar-School, and made to "do" fifty lines of Ovid a day.

The old belief that to translate Latin with facility was the true test of genius has fallen somewhat into desuetude, yet there are a few who still hold to the idea that to reason, imagine and invent are not the tests of a man's powers; he must conjugate, decline and derive. But Grant Allen, possessor of three college degrees, avers that a man may not even be able to read and write, and yet have a very firm mental grasp on the eternal verities.

Anyway, Joshua Reynolds did not like Latin. He hated the set task of fifty lines, and hated the system that imposed a fine of twenty lines for a failure to fulfil the first ⚜ ⚜

The fines piled up until young Joshua, aged twelve, goin' on thirteen, went into such hopeless bankruptcy that he could not pay tuppence on the pound.

We have a sheet of this Latin done at that time, in a cramped, schoolboy hand, starting very bold and plain, and running off into a tired blot and scrawl. On the bottom of the page is a picture, and under this is a line

JOSHUA REYNOLDS

written by the father: "This is drawn by Joshua in school out of pure idleness." The Reverend Samuel had no idea that his own name would live in history simply because he was the father of this idle boy.

Still, the clergyman showed that he was a man of good sense, for he acceded to the lad's request to let the Latin slide. This conclusion no doubt was the easier arrived at after the master of the school had explained that the proper education of such a youth was quite hopeless

All the Reynolds children drew pictures and most of them drew better than Joshua. But Joshua did not get along well at school, and so he felt the necessity of doing something

It is a great blessing to be born into a family where strict economy of time and money is necessary. The idea that nothing shall be wasted, and that each child must carve out for himself a career, is a thrice-blessed heritage

Rich parents are an awful handicap to youth, and few indeed there be who have the strength to stand prosperity; especially is this true when prosperity is not achieved, but thrust upon them.

Joshua got hold of a copy of Richardson's "Theory of Painting," and found therein that the author prophesied the rise of a great school of English painters.

Joshua thought about it, talked with his brothers and sisters about it, and surprised his mother by asking her

JOSHUA REYNOLDS

if she knew that there was soon to be a distinct school of British Art.

About this time there came to the village a strolling artist by the name of Warmell. This man opened up a studio on the porch of the tavern and offered to make your picture while you wait. He did a thriving business in silhouettes, and patrons who were in a hurry could have their profiles cut out of black paper with shears and pasted on a white background in a jiffy—price, sixpence ✼ ✼

Joshua struck up quite a friendship with this man and was taught all the tricks of the trade—even to the warning that in drawing the portrait of a homely man it is not good policy to make a really homely picture ✼

The best-paying pewholder in the Reverend Samuel Reynolds' church was a Mr. Craunch, whose picture had been made by the joint efforts of the strolling artist Warmell and young Reynolds. 'T was a very beautiful picture, although it is not on record that Mr. Craunch was a handsome man.

Warmell refused to take pay for Craunch's picture, claiming that he felt it was pay enough to have the honor of such a great man sitting to him. This remark proved to Craunch that Warmell was a discerning person and they were very soon on intimate terms of friendship. Mr. Craunch gave Mr. Warmell orders to paint pictures of the Craunch family. One day Warmell called the great man's attention to the fact that young

JOSHUA REYNOLDS

Reynolds, his volunteer assistant, had ambitions in an art way that could not be gratified unless some great and good man stepped in and played the part of a Mæcenas ✣ ✣

In fact, Joshua wanted to go to London and study with Hudson, the son-in-law and pupil of Richardson, the eminent author who wrote the "Theory of Painting." Warmell felt sure that after a few months, with his help, young Reynolds could get the technique and the color-scheme, and a' that, and the firm of Warmell and Reynolds could open a studio in Plymouth or Portsmouth and secure many good orders.

Craunch listened with patience and advised with the boy's parents.

The next week he took the lad up to London and entered him as a pupil with the great Hudson, who could not paint much of a picture himself, but for a consideration was willing to show others how.

Rumor has it that Warmell got a certain sum in English gold for all pupils he sent to Hudson's studio, but I take no stock in such insinuations.

Warmell here disappears from mortal view, like one of those stage trapdoor vanishings of Mephisto—only Mephisto usually comes back, but Warmell never did.

¶ Reynolds was very happy at Hudson's studio. He was only seventeen years old when he arrived there, fresh from the country. London was a marvel of delight to Joshua; the shops, theaters, galleries and exhibitions were a never-ending source of joy. He worked with diligence, and probably got more for his money than any one of Hudson's fifty pupils. Hudson was well-to-do, dignified and kind. His place was full of casts and classic fragments, and when he had set his pupils to copying these he considered his day's work done.

Joshua wrote glowing letters home, telling of all he did. "While I am at work I am the happiest creature alive," he said. Hudson set Joshua to copying Guercino's works, and kept the lad at it so steadily that he was really never able to draw from Nature correctly thereafter ✄

After a year, Craunch came up from the country to see how his ward was getting along. Joshua showed him the lions of the city; and painted his picture, making so fine a portrait that when Mr. Craunch got back home he threw away the one made by Warmell.

Once at an exhibition Joshua met Alexander Pope, whom he had seen several times at Hudson's studio. Pope remembered him and shook hands. Joshua was so inflated by the honor that he hastened home to write a letter to his mother and tell her all about it.

According to the terms of agreement with Hudson, Joshua was bound to stay four years; but now two years had passed, and one fine day in sudden wrath Hudson told him to pack up his kit and go.

The trouble was that Joshua could paint better than Hudson—every pupil in the school knew it. When the scholars wanted advice they went to Reynolds, and

JOSHUA REYNOLDS

some of them, being sons of rich men, paid Reynolds for helping them.
Then Reynolds had painted a few portraits on his own account and had kept the money, as he had a perfect right to do. Hudson said he had n't, for he was bound as an apprentice to him.
"But only during working-hours," replied young Reynolds. We can hardly blame Hudson for sending him away—no master wants a pupil around who sees all over, above and beyond him, and who can do better work than he. It's confusing, and tends to rob the master of the deification that is his due.
Reynolds had remained long enough—it was time for him to go.
He went back to Devonshire, and Craunch, the biggest man in Plympton, took him over to Lord Edgecumbe, the biggest man in Plymouth.
Craunch carried along the portrait of himself that Joshua had made, and asked milord if he did n't want one just like it. Edgecumbe said he surely did, and asked Joshua if he painted the picture all alone by himself ⚹ Joshua smiled.
Lord Edgecumbe had a beautiful house, and to have a good picture of himself, and a few choice old ancestors on the walls, he thought would be very fine.
Joshua took up his abode in the Edgecumbe mansion, the better to do his work.
He was a handsome youth, nearly twenty years old,

JOSHUA REYNOLDS

with bright, beaming eyes, a slight but compact form, and brown curls that came to his shoulders. His London life had given him a confidence in himself, and in his manner there was a grace and poise flavored with a becoming diffidence.

A man who can do things well should assume a modesty, even if he has it not. If you can write well, do not talk—leave that to the man who can do nothing else. If you can paint, let your work speak for you.

Joshua Reynolds was young, but he was an artist in diplomacy. His talent, his modesty, his youth, his beauty, won the hearts of the entire Edgecumbe household.

He painted portraits of all the family; and of course all the visitors were called upon to admire, not only the pictures, but the painter as well.

A studio was opened in one of Lord Edgecumbe's buildings at Plymouth, and he painted portraits of all the great folks thereabout.

On Christmas-Day, Seventeen Hundred Forty-six, the Reverend Samuel Reynolds died, but before his death he fully realized that one of his children was well on the way to fame and fortune.

The care of the broken family now devolved on Joshua, but his income was several times as much as his father had ever earned, and his responsibilities were carried lightly.

While at the house of Lord Edgecumbe, Reynolds had

JOSHUA REYNOLDS

met young Commodore Keppel. In Seventeen Hundred Forty-nine, Keppel was placed in command of the Mediterranean fleet, with orders to clear the seas of the Barbary pirates. Keppel invited Reynolds to join him on board the " Centurion " as his guest.

Gladly he accepted, and they sailed away for the Orient with a cabin stocked with good things, and enough brushes, paints, canvases and easels to last several painters a lifetime.

JOSHUA REYNOLDS

T was three years before Reynolds came back to Plymouth. He had visited Lisbon, Cadiz, Gibraltar, Port Mahon and Minorca. At the two last-named places there were British garrisons, and Reynolds set to work making portraits of the officers. For this he was so well paid that he decided to visit Italy instead of voyaging farther with his friend Keppel.

He then journeyed on to Naples, Rome, Venice, Pisa and Florence, stopping in each city for several months, immersing himself in the art atmosphere of the place. Returning to Rome, he remained there two years, studying and copying the works of Raphael, Angelo, Titian and other masters.

Occasionally, he sold his copies of masterpieces, and by practising strict economy managed to live in a fair degree of comfort.

Rome is the hottest place in Summer and the coldest in Winter of which I know. The average Italian house has a damp and chill in Winter which clutches the tourist and makes him long for home and native land. Imagine a New England farmhouse in March with only a small dish-pan of coals to warm it, and you have Rome in Winter ⚜ ⚜

Rome, with its fever in Summer and rheumatism and pneumonia in Winter, has sent many an artist to limbus. Joshua Reynolds escaped the damp of the Vatican with nothing worse than a deafness that caused him to carry

JOSHUA REYNOLDS

an ear-trumpet for the rest of his life. ¶ But now he was back at Plymouth. Lord Edgcumbe looked over the work he had brought and called into the ear-trumpet that a man who could paint like that was a fool to remain in a country town: he should go to London and vanquish all such alleged artists as Hudson.

Keppel had gotten back to England, and he and Edgcumbe had arranged that Reynolds should pitch his tent in the heart of artistic London. So a handsome suite of apartments was secured in Saint Martin's Lane.
¶ The first work undertaken seems to have been that full-length portrait of Commodore Keppel. The picture shows the Commodore standing on a rocky shore, issuing orders to unseen hosts. There is an energy, dash and heroism pictured in the work that at once caught the eye of the public.

" Have you seen Keppel's portrait? " asked Edgcumbe of every one he met.

Invitations were sent out to call at Joshua Reynold's studio and see " Keppel." There were a good many pictures displayed there, but " Keppel " was placed in a small room, set apart, rightly focused, properly draped, and lighted only by candles, that stood in silver candlesticks, and which were solemnly snuffed by a detailed marine, six foot three, in a red coat, with a formidable hanger at his side. Only a few persons were admitted at a time and on entering the room all you saw was the valiant form of the doughty Commodore, the sea-mist in his face and the wild winds blowing his locks. The big marine on guard in the shadow added the last realistic touch, and the gentlemen visitors removed their hats and the ladies talked in whispers—they all expected Keppel to speak, and they wished to hear what he would say.

It is a great thing to paint a beautiful picture, but 't is a more difficult feat to hypnotize the public into accepting the fact.

The live Keppel was pointed out on the street as the man who had had his picture taken.

Now, people do not have portraits painted simply because they want portraits painted: they want these portraits shown and admired.

To have Reynolds paint your portrait might prove a repetition of the Keppel—who knows!

Sitters came and a secretary in livery took their names and made appointments, as is done today in the office of a prosperous dentist.

Joshua Reynolds was young and strong, and he worked while it was called the day. He worked from sunrise until sunset.

That first year in London he produced one hundred twenty portraits, besides painting various other pictures. This he could not have done without the assistance of a most loyal helper.

This helper was Giuseppe Marchi.

There are a half-dozen biographies of Reynolds, and

JOSHUA REYNOLDS

from Boswell, Walpole and Burney, Gossips-in-Ordinary, we have vivid glimpses into his life and habits. Then we have his own journal, and hundreds of letters; but nowhere do we get a frank statement of the assistance rendered him by Giuseppe Marchi.

When Reynolds was in Rome, aged twenty-one, he fell in with a tatterdemalion, who proffered his service as guide. Rome is full of such specimens, and the type is one that has not changed in five hundred years.

Reynolds tossed the lad a copper, and the ragged one showed his fine white teeth in a gladsome grin and proffered information. He clung to the visitor all that afternoon, and the next morning when Reynolds started out with his sketching-outfit, the youngster was sitting on his doorstep. So they fared forth, Giuseppe carrying the kit ✄ ✄

Reynolds knew but little Italian—the boy taught him more. The boy knew every corner of Rome, and was deep in the history of the Eternal City—all he knew was Rome ✄ ✄

Joshua taught the youngster to sketch, and after the first few days there in Rome, Joshua rigged Giuseppe up an easel, and where went Joshua there also went Giuseppe ✄ ✄

Joshua got a bit ashamed of his partner's attire and bought him better raiment.

When Reynolds left Rome on his homeward march, there, too, tagged the faithful Giuseppe.

JOSHUA REYNOLDS

After several months they reached Lyons, and Joshua counted his money. There was only enough to pay his fare by the diligence to Paris, with a few francs over for food. He told Giuseppe that he could not take him farther, and emptying his pockets of all his coppers, and giving him his best silk handkerchief and a sketching-outfit, they cried down each other's backs, kissed each other on both cheeks in the Italian fashion, and parted.
¶ It took eight days to reach Paris by the diligence, and Joshua only got through by stopping one day and bartering a picture for sundry loaves of necessary bread.
¶ But he had friends in Paris, influential friends. And when he reached the home of these influential friends, there on the curbstone sat Giuseppe, awaiting his coming, with the silk handkerchief knotted loosely about his neck!
Giuseppe had thrown away the painting-kit and walked the three hundred miles in eight days, begging or stealing by the way the food he needed.
When Joshua Reynolds opened his studio in Saint Martin's Lane, his faithful helper was Giuseppe Marchi. Giuseppe painted just as Joshua did, and just as well.
¶ When sitters came, Giuseppe was only a valet: he cleaned the brushes, polished the knives, ran for water and hovered near to do his master's bidding. He was the only person allowed in the model-room, and all the time he was there his keen eyes made a correct and proper estimate of the sitter. Listening to no conversation,

JOSHUA REYNOLDS

seeing nothing, he yet heard everything and nothing escaped his glance.

When the sitting, which occupied an hour, was over, Giuseppe took the picture into another room and filled in the background and drapery just as he knew it should be ※ ※

"Marchi does not sign and date the portraits, but he does all the rest," said Garrick. And "Little Burney," treading on thinner ice, once remarked, "If Sir Joshua ever embraces a fair sitter and imprints upon her forehead a chaste kiss, I am sure that Giuseppe Marchi will never tell."

It is too late to accuse Sir Joshua Reynolds of ingratitude towards Giuseppe; he was grateful, and once referred to Marchi as "an angel sent from God to help me do my work." But he paid Marchi valet's wages and treated him like a servant. Possibly this was the part of expedience, for had Marchi ever gotten it into his head that he could paint as well as Sir Joshua he would have been worthless as a helper.

For forty years they were never separated.

Cotton disposes of Giuseppe Marchi by saying, "He was a clever colorist, but incapable of doing independent work." Cotton might, however, have told the whole simple truth, and that was that Marchi was hands, feet, eyes and ears for his master—certain it is that without his help Sir Joshua could never have attained the fame and fortune he did.

JOSHUA REYNOLDS

N selecting his time for a career, Joshua Reynolds showed good judgment. He went into public favor on a high tide. England was prosperous, and there was in the air a taste for the polite arts. Literature was becoming a fad. ¶ Within a short time there had appeared Gray's " Elegy," Smollett's " Peregrine Pickle," Fielding's " Amelia " and Richardson's " Clarissa Harlowe." Here was menu to fit most palates, and the bill-of-fare was duly discussed in all social gatherings of the upper circles. The afflicted ones fed on Gray; the repentant quoted Richardson; while Smollett and Fielding were read aloud in parlor gatherings where fair ladies threatened to leave the room—but did n't. Out at Strawberry Hill, his country home, Horace Walpole was running that little printing-shop, making books that are now priceless, and writing long, gossipy letters that body forth the spirit of the time, its form and pressure. The Dilettante Society, composed of young noblemen devoted to high art and good-fellowship, was discussing a scheme for a National Academy. Garrick was at the height of his fame; Hogarth was doing for art what Smollett did for literature; while two young Irishmen, Burke and Goldsmith, were getting ready to make English letters illustrious; Hudson was painting portraits with a stencil; Gainsborough was immortalizing a hat; Doctor Johnson was waiting in the entry of Lord Chesterfield's mansion with the prospectus of a

JOSHUA REYNOLDS

dictionary; and pretty Kitty Fisher had kicked the hat off the head of the Prince of Wales on a wager.
And so into this atmosphere of seething life came Joshua Reynolds, the handsome, gracious, silent, diplomatic Reynolds. Fresh from Italy and the far-off islands of the Southern seas where Ulysses sailed, he came—his name and fame heralded as the Raphael of England.
To have your portrait painted by Reynolds was considered a proper "entree" into the "bon ton." To attempt to give the names of royalty who sat to him would be to present a transcript of Burke's Peerage.
Unlike Van Dyck, at whose shrine Reynolds worshiped, Reynolds was coldly diplomatic in his relations with his sitters. He talked but little, because he could not hear, and to hold an ear-trumpet and paint with both hands is rather difficult. On the moment when the sitting was over, the patron was bowed out. The good ladies who lay in wait with love's lariat never found an opportunity to make the throw.
Reynolds' specialty was women and children. No man has ever pictured them better, and with him all women were kind. Not only were they good, but good-looking; and when arms lacked contour, or busts departed from the ideal, Kitty Fisher or Nelly O'Brien came at the call of Marchi and lent their charms to complete the canvas.
Reynolds gradually raised his prices until he received fifteen guineas for a head, one hundred for a half-length,

JOSHUA REYNOLDS

and one hundred and fifty for a full-length. And so rapidly did he work that often a picture was completed in four hours.

Usually, success is a zigzag journey, but it was not so with Reynolds. From Seventeen Hundred Fifty-seven to Seventeen Hundred Eighty-eight, his income was never less than thirty thousand dollars a year, and his popularity knew no eclipse.

About the time the American Stamp Act was being pushed through Parliament, Reynolds' studio was the neutral stamping-ground for both parties.

Copley, the Boston artist, gave Reynolds a bias in favor of truth; and when Townshend, the man who introduced the Stamp Act in Parliament, sat to Sir Joshua, the artist and sitter forgot their business and wrangled over politics. Soon afterward Sir Joshua made a bet with Townshend, a thousand pounds against five, that George Washington would never enter Reynolds' studio. This was in response to the boast that Washington would soon be brought to England a captive, and Townshend would conduct him to Reynolds to have his picture taken.

The bet made a sensation and Reynolds offered to repeat it to all comers; and a score or more of sincere men paid over five pounds into the hands of Sir Joshua, and took his note for one thousand pounds, payable when Washington landed in England a prisoner.

Old Ursa Major had small patience with Reynolds'

JOSHUA REYNOLDS

political prophecies; he called America a land of pirates and half-breed cutthroats, and would have bet Sir Joshua to a standstill—only he had conscientious scruples about betting, and besides, had n't any money. ¶ Goldsmith and Burke, of course, sided with Reynolds in his American sympathies, and Garrick referred to them as " My friends, the three Irish Gentlemen." A frequent visitor at the studio at this time was Angelica Kauffman, who deserves a volume instead of a mere mention. She came up from Switzerland, unknown, and made her way to the highest artistic circles in London. She had wit and beauty, and painted so well that Reynolds admitted she taught him a few tricks in the use of color. She produced several portraits of Reynolds, and Reynolds painted several of her; and the daughter of Thackeray wrote a novel which turns on the assumption that they were lovers.

There certainly was a fine comradeship existing between them; but whether Reynolds was ever capable of an all-absorbing passion there is much doubt. He was married to his work.

Reynolds had many intimate friends among women: Peg Woffington, Mrs. Clive, Mrs. Thrale, Hannah More, Fanny Burney and others. With them all there went the same high, chivalrous and generous disinterestedness. He was a friend to each in very fact.

When the Royal Academy was formed in Seventeen Hundred Sixty-eight, Reynolds was made its president,

JOSHUA REYNOLDS

and this office he held until the close of his life. He was not one of the chief promoters of the Academy at the beginning, and the presidency was half forced upon him. He might have declined the honor then had the King not made him a knight, and showed that it was his wish that Reynolds should accept. Sir Joshua, however, had more ballast in his character than any other painter of his time, and it was plain that without his name at the head the Academy would be a thing for smiles and quiet jokes.

The thirty-four charter members included the names of two Americans, Copley and West, and of one woman, Angelica Kauffman.

And it is here worthy of note that although the Methodist Church still refuses to allow women to sit as delegates in its General Conference, yet, in Seventeen Hundred Sixty-eight, no dissent was made when Joshua Reynolds suggested the name of a woman as a member of the Royal Academy.

Sir Joshua did not forget his friends at the time honors were given out, for he secured the King's permission to add several honorary members to the Academy—men who could n't paint, but who still expressed themselves well in other ways.

Doctor Johnson was made Professor of Ancient Literature; Oliver Goldsmith, Professor of Ancient History; and Richard Dalton, Librarian.

In this case the office did not seek the man: the man was

JOSHUA REYNOLDS

duly measured, and the office manufactured to fit him.
¶ When Sir Joshua died, in February, Seventeen Hundred Ninety-two, it was the close of a success so uninterrupted that it seems unequaled in the history of art. He left a fortune equal to considerably more than half a million dollars; he had contributed valuable matter to the cause of literature; he had been the earnest friend of all workers in the cause of letters, music and art; and had also been the intimate adviser and confidant of royalty. He was generous and affectionate, wise and sincere; a cheerful and tireless worker—one in whom the elements were so well mixed that all the world might say, This was a man!

LANDSEER

LANDSEER

The man behind his work was seen through it—sensitive, variously gifted, manly, genial, tender-hearted, simple and unaffected; a lover of animals, children and humanity; and if any one wishes to see at a glance nearly all we have written, let him look at Landseer's portrait, painted by himself, with a canine connoisseur on either side.

—Monkhouse

LANDSEER

APPY lives make dull biographies. Young women with ambitions should be very cautious lest mayhap they be caught in the soft, silken mesh of a happy marriage, and go down to oblivion, dead to the world.
"Miss Pott—the beautiful Miss Pott," they called her. The biographers did n't take time to give her first name, nor recount her pedigree, so rapt were they with her personality. They only say, "She was tall, willowy and lissome; and Sir Joshua Reynolds painted her picture as a peasant beauty, bearing on her well-poised head a sheaf of corn."
It was at the house of Macklin, the rich publisher, that John Landseer, the engraver, met Miss Pott. She was artistic in all her instincts; and as she knew the work of the brilliant engraver and named his best pieces without hesitation he grew interested. Men grow interested when you know and appreciate their work; sometimes they grow more interested, at which time they are also interesting ⚜ ⚜
And so it came about that they were married, the beautiful Miss Pott and John Landseer, and it can also be truthfully added that they were happy ever afterward ⚜ ⚜

LANDSEER

But that was the last of Miss Pott. Her husband was so strong, so self-centered, so capable, that he protected her from every fierce wind, and gratified her every wish. She believed in him thoroughly and conformed her life to his. Her personality was lost in him. The biographer scarcely refers to her, save when he is obliged to, indirectly, to record that she became the mother of three fine girls, and the same number of boys, equally fine, by name, Thomas, Charles and Edwin.

Thomas and Charles grew to be strong, learned and useful men, so accomplished in literature and art that their names would shine bright on history's page, were they not thrown into the shadow by the youngest brother ⚜ ⚜

Before Edwin Landseer was twenty years of age he was known throughout the United Kingdom as "Landseer." John Landseer was known as "the father of Landseer," and the others were "the brothers of Landseer."

And when once in Piccadilly, the beautiful Miss Pott (that was) was pointed out as "the mother of Landseer," the words warmed the heart of the good woman like wine. To be the wife of a great man, and the mother of a greater was career enough—she was very happy.

Queen Anne Street, near Cavendish Square, is a shabby district, with long lines of plain brick houses built for revenue only.

But Queen Anne Street is immortal to all lovers of art because it was the home of Turner; and within its dark,

LANDSEER

dull and narrow confines were painted the most dazzlingly beautiful canvases that the world has ever seen. And yet again the street has another claim on our grateful remembrance, for at Number Eighty-three was born, on March Seventh, Eighteen Hundred Two, Edwin Landseer.

The father of Landseer was an enthusiastic lover of art. He had sprung from a long line of artistic workers in precious metals; and to use a pencil with skill he regarded as the chief end of man.

Long before his children knew their letters, they were taught to make pictures. Indeed, all children can make pictures before they can write. For a play-spell, each day John Landseer and his boys tramped across Hampstead Heath to where there were donkeys, sheep, goats and cows grazing; then all four would sit down on the grass before some chosen subject and sketch the patient model.

Edwin Landseer's first loving recollections of his father went back to these little excursions across the Heath. And for each boy to take back to his mother and sisters a picture of something they had seen was a great joy ⚜ " Well, boys, what shall we draw today? " the father would ask at breakfast-time.

And then they would all vote on it, and arguments in favor of goat or donkey were eloquently and skilfully set forth.

I said that a very young child could draw pictures:

LANDSEER

standing by my chair as I write this line is a chubby little girl, just four years old, in a check dress, with two funny little braids down her back. She is begging me for this pencil that she may " make a pussy-cat for Mamma to put in a frame."

What boots it that the little girl's " pussy-cat " has five or six legs and three tails—these are all inferior details. The evolution of the individual mirrors the evolution of the race, and long before races began to write or reason they made pictures.

Art education had better begin young, for then it is a sort of play; and good artistic work, Robert Louis Stevenson once said, is only useful play.

Probably Edwin Landseer's education began a hundred years before he was born; but his technical instruction in art began when he was three years old, when his father would take him out on the Heath and placing him on the grass, put pencil and paper in his hand and let him make a picture of a goat nibbling the grass.

Then the boy noted for himself that a goat had a short tail, a cow a switch-tail, and horses had no horns, and that a ram's horns were unlike those of a goat.

He had begun to differentiate and compare—and not yet four years old!

When five years of age he could sketch a sleeping dog as it lay on the floor better than could Thomas, his brother, who was seven years older.

We know the deep personal interest that John Landseer

LANDSEER

felt in the boy, for he preserved his work, and today in the South Kensington Museum we can see a series of sketches made by Edwin Landseer, running from his fifth year to manhood.

Thus do we trace the unfolding of his genius.

That young Landseer's drawing was a sort of play there is no doubt. People who set very young children at tasks of grubbing out cold facts from books come plainly within the province of the Society for the Prevention of Cruelty to Animals, and should be looked after, but to do things with one's hands for fun is only a giving direction to the natural energies.

Before Edwin Landseer was eight years of age his father had taught him the process of etching, and we see that even then the lad had a vivid insight into the character of animals. He drew pictures of pointers, mastiffs, spaniels and bulldogs, and gave to each the right expression 🙢 🙢

The Landseers owned several dogs, and what they did not own they borrowed; and once we know that Charles and Thomas "borrowed" a mastiff without the owner's consent.

All children go through the scissors age, when they cut out of magazines, newspapers or books all the pictures they can find, so as to add to the "collection." Often these youthful collectors have specialties: one will collect pictures of animals, another of machinery, and still another of houses. But usually it is animals that

LANDSEER

attract. ¶ Scissors were forbidden in the Landseer household, and if the boys wanted pictures they had to make them.
And they made them.
They drew horses, sheep, donkeys, cattle, dogs; and when their father took them to the Zoological Garden it was only that they might bring back trophies in the way of lions and tigers.
Then we find that there was once a curiosity exhibited in Fleet Street in the way of a lion-cub that had been caught in Africa and mothered by a Newfoundland dog. The old mother-dog thought just as much of the orphan that was placed among her brood as of her sure-enough children. The owner had never allowed the two animals to be separated, and when the lion had grown to be twice the size of his foster-mother there still existed between the two a fine affection.
The stepmother exercised a stepmother's rights, and occasionally chastised, for his own good, her overgrown charge, and the big brute would whimper and whine like a lubberly boy.
This curious pair of animals made a great impression on the Landseers. The father and three boys sketched them in various attitudes, and engravings of Edwin's sketch are still to be had.
And so wherever in London animals were to be found, there, too, were the Landseers with pencils and brushes, and pads and palettes.

LANDSEER

In the back yard of the house where the Landseers lived were sundry pens of pet rabbits; in the attic were pigeons, and dogs of various breeds lay on the doorstep sleeping in the sun, or barked at you out of the windows. ¶ It is reported that John Landseer once contemplated a change of residence; he selected the house he wanted, bargained with the landlord, agreed as to terms and handed out his card preparatory to signing a lease. The real-estate agent looked at the name, stuttered, stammered, and finally said: "You must excuse me, Sir, but they say as how you are a dealer in dogs, and your boys are dog-catchers! You'll excuse me—but—I just now 'appened to think the 'ouse is already took!"

LANDSEER

HE Landseers moved from Queen Anne Street to Foley Street, near Burlington House. This was a neighborhood of artists, and for neighbors they had West, Mulready, Northcote, Constable, Flaxman and our own picturesque Allston, of Cambridge, Massachusetts.

The Elgin Marbles were then kept at Burlington House, and these were a great source of inspiration to the Landseer boys. It gave them a true taste of the Grecian, and knowing a little about Greece, they wanted to know more. Greece became the theme—they talked it at breakfast, dinner and supper. The father and mother told them all they knew, and guessed at a few things more, and to keep at least one lesson ahead of the children the parents "crammed for examination." Edwin sketched that world-famous horse's head from the Parthenon, and the figures of horses and animals in bas-relief that formed the frieze; and the boys figured out in their minds why horses and men were all the same height.

Gradually it dawned upon the father and the brothers that Edwin was their master so far as drawing was concerned. They could sketch a Newfoundland dog that would pass for anybody's Newfoundland, but Edwin's was a certain identical dog, and none other.

Edwin Landseer really discovered the dog.

He discovered that dogs of one breed may be very different in temper and disposition; and going further

LANDSEER

he found that dogs have character and personality. He struck an untouched lode and worked it out to his own delight and the delight of great numbers of others.

His pictures were not mystical, profound or problematic—simply dogs, but dogs with feelings, affections, jealousies, prejudices. In short, he showed that dogs, after all, are very much like folks; and from this, people with a turn for psychology reasoned that the source of life in the dog was the same as the source of life in man.
¶ Plain people who owned a dog beloved by the whole household, as household dogs always are, became interested in Landseer's dogs. They could not buy a painting by Landseer, but they could spare a few shillings for an engraving.

And so John Landseer began to reproduce the pictures of Edwin's dogs.

The demand grew, and Thomas now ceased to sketch and devoted all his time to etching and engraving his brother's work.

Every one knew of Landseer, even people who cared nothing for art: they wanted a picture of one of his dogs to hang over the chimney, because the dog looked like one they used to own.

Then rich people came and wanted Edwin to paint a portrait of their dog, and a studio was opened where the principal sitters were dogs. From a position where close economy must be practised, the Landseers found themselves with more money than they knew what to do with.

LANDSEER

Edwin was barely twenty, but had exhibited at several Royal Academy Exhibitions and his name was on every tongue. He gave no attention to marketing his wares—his father and brothers did all that—he simply sketched and had a good time. He was healthy, strong, active, and could walk thirty miles a day; but now that riches had come that way he bought a horse and rode. Then other horses were presented to him, and he began to picture horses, too. That he knew horses and loved them is evidenced in many a picture. In every village or crossroads town of America can be found copies of his "Shoeing," where stands the sleek bay mare, the sober, serious donkey, and the big dog.

No painter who ever lived is so universally known as Landseer, and this is because his father and brothers made it their life-business to reproduce his work by engraving.

Occasionally, rich ladies would want their own portraits painted with a favorite dog at their feet, or men wanted themselves portrayed on horseback, and so Landseer found himself with more orders than he could well care for. People put their names, or the name of their dog, on his waiting-list, and some of the dogs died of old age before the name was reached.

"I hear," said a lady to Sydney Smith at a dinner party—"I hear you are to have your portrait painted by Landseer."

"Is thy servant a dog that he should do this thing?"

LANDSEER

answered the wit. ¶ The story went the rounds, and Mulready once congratulated the clergyman on the repartee ❧ ❧
" I never made the reply," said Sydney Smith; " but I wish I had."
Sydney Smith was once visiting the Landseer studio, and his eye chanced to light on the picture of a very peculiar-looking dog.
" Yes, it's a queer picture of a queer dog. The drawing is bad enough, and never pleased me!" And Landseer picked up the picture and gave it a toss out of the window. " You may have it if you care to go get it," he carelessly remarked to the visitor. Smith made haste to run downstairs and out of the house to secure his prize. He found it lodged in the branches of a tree.
In telling the tale years afterward, Smith remarked that, whereas many men had climbed trees to evade dogs, yet he alone of all men had once climbed a tree to secure one.
¶ Sir Walter Scott saw Landseer's picture of " The Cat's Paw," and was so charmed with it that he hunted out the young artist, and soon after invited him to Abbotsford ❧ ❧
Leslie, the American artist, was at that time at Scott's home painting the novelist's portrait. This portrait, by the way, became the property of the Ticknor family of Boston, and was exhibited a few years ago at the Boston Museum of Fine Arts.
Landseer, Leslie and Scott made a choice trio of

LANDSEER

congenial spirits. They were all " outdoor men," strong, sturdy, good-natured, and fond of boyish romp and frolic. Many were the long tramps they took across mountain, heath and heather. They visited the Highland district together, fished in Loch Lomond, paddled the entire length of Loch Katrine, and hunted deer on the preserve of Lord Gwydr.

On one hunting excursion, Landseer was stationed on a runway, gun in hand, with a gillie in attendance. The dogs started a fine buck, which ran close to them, but instead of leveling his gun, Landseer shoved the weapon into the hands of the astonished gillie with the hurried whispered request, " Here, you, hold this for me! " and seizing his pencil, made a hasty sketch of the gallant buck ere the vision could fade from memory.

In fact, both Landseer and Leslie proved poor sportsmen—they had no heart for killing things.

A beautiful live deer was a deal more pleasing to Landseer than a dead one; and he might truthfully have expressed the thought of his mind by saying, " A bird in the bush is worth two on a woman's bonnet." And indeed he did anticipate Thoreau by saying, " To shoot a bird is to lose it."

The idea of following deer with dogs and guns, simply for the sport of killing them, was repugnant to the soul of this sensitive, tender-hearted man.

In the faces of his deer he put a look of mingled grandeur and pain—a half-pathos, as if foreshadowing their fate.

LANDSEER

In picturing the dogs and donkeys, he was full of jest and merriment; but the kings of moor and forest called forth deeper and sadder sentiments.

That wild animals instinctively flee in frenzied alarm at man's approach is comment enough on our treatment of them ❧ ❧

The deer, so gentle and so graceful, so innocent and so beautiful, are never followed by man except as a destroyer; and the idea of looking down a rifle-barrel into the wide-open, soulful eyes of a deer made Landseer sick at heart.

LANDSEER

O Landseer must be given the honor of first opening a friendly communication between the present royal family and the artistic and literary world.

Wild-eyed poets and rusty-looking, impecunious painters were firmly warned away from Balmoral. The thought that all poets and painters were anarchistic and dangerous—certainly disagreeable—was firmly fixed in the heart of the young Queen and her attendants.

The barrier had first been raised to Landseer. He was requested to visit the palace and paint a picture of one of the Queen's deerhounds. It was found that the man was not hirsute, untamed or eccentric. He was a gentleman in manner and education—quite self-contained and manly.

He was introduced to the Queen; they shook hands and talked about dogs and horses and things, just like old acquaintances. They loved the same things, and so were friends at once. It was not long before Landseer's near neighbors at Saint John's Wood were stricken speechless at the spectacle of Queen Victoria on horseback waiting at the door of Landseer's house, while the artist ran in to change his coat. When he came out he mounted one of the groom's horses for a gallop across the park with the Queen of England, on whose possessions the sun never sets.

These rides with royalty were, however, largely a matter of professional study; for he not only painted a picture

LANDSEER

of the Queen on horseback, but of Albert as well. And at Windsor there can now be seen many pictures of dogs and horses painted by Landseer, with nobility incidentally introduced, or vice versa, if you prefer.

It was in Eighteen Hundred Thirty-five that Landseer began to paint the pets of the royal family, and the friendly intimacy then begun continued up to the time of his death in Eighteen Hundred Seventy-three.

In the National Academy are sixty-seven canvases by Landseer; and for the Queen, personally, he completed over one hundred pictures, for which he received a sum equal to a quarter of a million dollars.

Landseer's career was one of continuous prosperity. In his life there was neither tragedy nor disappointment. His horses and dogs filled his bachelor heart, and when Tray, Blanche and Sweetheart bayed and barked him a welcome to that home in Saint John's Wood where he lived for just fifty years, he was supremely content. His fortune of three hundred thousand pounds was distributed at his death, as he requested, among various servants, friends and needy kinsmen.

Landseer had no enemies, and no detractors worth mentioning. That his great popularity was owing to his deference to the spirit of the age goes without saying. He never affronted popular prejudices, and was ever alert to reflect the taste of his patrons. The influence of passing events was strong upon him: the subtlety of Turner, the spiritual vision of Fra Angelico, the sublime

LANDSEER

quality of soul (that scorned present reward and dedicated its work to time) of Michelangelo were all far from him.

That he at times attempted to be humorous by dressing dogs in coats and trousers with pipe in mouth is to be regretted. A dog so clothed is not funny—the artist is ※
The point has also been made that in Landseer's work there was no progression—no evolution. His pictures of mountain scenery done in Scotland before he was thirty mark high tide. To him never again came the same sweep of joyous spirit or surge of feeling.

Bank-accounts, safety and satisfaction are not the things that stir the emotions and sound the soul-depths. Landseer never knew the blessing of a noble discontent. But he contributed to the quiet joy of a million homes; and it is not for us to say, " It is beautiful; but is it art? " Neither need we ask whether the name of Landseer will endure with those of Raphael and Leonardo. Edwin Landseer did a great work, and the world is better for his having lived; for his message was one of gentleness, kindness and beauty.

GUSTAVE DORE

GUSTAVE DORE

Lacroix told Dore one day, early in his life in Paris, that he should illustrate a new edition of his works in four volumes, and he sent them to him. In a week Lacroix said to Dore, who had called, " Well, have you begun to read my story? " " Oh! I mastered that in no time; the blocks are all ready "; and while Lacroix looked on stupefied, the boy dived into his pockets and piled many of them on the table, saying, " The others are in a basket at the door; there are three hundred in all! "
—*Blanche Roosevelt*

GUSTAVE DORE

IT was at the Cafe de l'Horloge in Paris. Mr. Whistler sat leaning on his cane, looking off into space, dreamily and wearily.
He roused enough to answer the question: "Dore—Gustave Dore—an artist? Why, the name sounds familiar! Oh, yes, an illustrator. Ah, now I understand; but there is a difference between an artist and an illustrator, you know, my boy. Dore—yes, I knew him—he had bats in his belfry!"
And Mr. Whistler dismissed the subject by calling for a match, and then smoked his cigarette in grim silence, blowing the smoke through his nose.
Not liking a man, it is easy to shelve him with a joke, or to waive his work with a shrug and toss of the head, but not always will the ghost down at our bidding ❧
In the realm of art nothing is more strange than this: genius does not recognize genius. Still, the word is much abused, and the man who is a genius to some is never so to others. In defining a genius it is easiest to work by the rule of elimination and show what he is not.
For instance, neither Reynolds, Landseer nor Meissonier was a genius. These men were strong, sane, well poised—filled with energy and life. They were receptive and quick to grasp a suggestion or hint that could be turned

GUSTAVE DORE

to their advantage—to further the immediate plans they had in hand. They had ambition and the ability to concentrate on a thing and do it. Just what they focused their attention upon was largely a matter of accident. They had in them the capacity for success—they could have succeeded at anything they undertook, and they were too sensible to undertake a thing at which they could not succeed. They always saw light through at the other end.

" I have success tied to the leg of my easel by a blue ribbon," said Meissonier.

They succeeded by mathematical calculation, and the fame, name and gold they won was through a conscious laying hold upon the laws that bring these things to pass.
¶ They chose to paint pictures, and the entire energy of their natures was concentrated upon this one thing. Practising the art, day after day, month after month, year after year, they acquired a wonderful facility. They knew the history of art—its failures, pitfalls and successes. They knew the human heart—they knew what the people wanted and what they did n't. They set themselves to supply a demand. And all this keenness, combined with good taste and tireless energy, would have brought a like success in any one of a dozen different professions.

And these are the men who give plausibility to that stern half-truth: a man can succeed in anything he undertakes—it is all a matter of will.

But you can not count Gustave Dore in any such category. He stands alone: he had no predecessors, and he left no successors. We say that the artist has his prototype; but every rule has its exception—even this one ✿ ✿

Gustave Dore drew pictures because he could do nothing else. He never had a lesson in his life, never drew from a model, could not sketch from Nature; accepted no one's advice; never retouched or considered his work after it was done; never cudgeled his brains for a subject; could read a book by turning the leaves; grasped all knowledge; knew all languages; found an immediate market for his wares and often earned a thousand dollars before breakfast; lived fifty years and produced over one hundred thousand sketches—an average of six a day; made two million dollars by the labor of his own hands; was knighted, flattered, proclaimed, adored, lauded, scorned, scoffed, hooted, maligned, and died broken-hearted.

Surely you can not dispose of a man like this with a "bon mot"!

Comets may be good or ill, but wise men nevertheless make note of them, and the fact that they once flashed their blinding light upon us must live in the history of things that were.

GUSTAVE DORE

N Alsatian by birth, and a Parisian by environment, Dore is spoken of as of the French School, but if ever an artist belonged to no " school " it was Gustave Dore.
His early years were spent in Strassburg, within the shadow of the cathedral. His father was a civil engineer —methodical, calculating, prosperous. The lad was the second of three sons: strong, bright, intelligent boys ✣ In his travels up and down the Rhine the father often took little Gustave with him, and the lad came to know each wild crag, and crowning fortress, and bend in the river where strong men with spears and bows and arrows used to lie in wait. In imagination Gustave repeopled the ruins and filled the weird forests with curious, haunting shapes. The Rhine reeks with history that merges off into misty song and fable; and this folklore of the storied river filled the day-dreams and night-dreams of this curious boy.

But all children have a vivid imagination, and the chief problem of modern education is how to conserve and direct it. As yet no scheme or plan or method has been devised that shows results, and the men of imagination seem to be those who have succeeded in spite of school. In Gustave Dore we have the curious spectacle of Nature keeping bright and fresh in the man all those strange conceptions of the child, and multiplying them by a man's strength.

The wild imaginings of Gustave only served his father

GUSTAVE DORE

and mother with food for laughter; and his erratic absurdities in making pictures supplied the neighbors' fun

But actions that are funny in a child become disturbing in a man; he's cute when little, but "sassy" when older

Gustave, however, did not put away childish things. When he had reached the age of indiscretion—was fourteen, and had a frog in his throat, and was conscious of being barefoot—he still imagined things and made pictures of them. His father was distressed, and sought by bribes to get him to quit scrawling with pencil and turn his attention to logarithms and other useful things; but with only partial success.

When fifteen he accompanied his father and older brother to Paris, where the older boy was to be installed in the Ecole Polytechnique. It was the hope of the father that, once in Paris, Gustave would consent to remain with his brother, and thus, by a change of base, a reform in his tastes would come about and he would leave the Rhine with its foolish old-woman tales and cease the detestable habit of picturing them.

It was the first time Gustave had ever been to Paris—the first time he had ever visited a large city. He was fascinated, captivated, enthralled. Paris was fairyland and paradise. He announced to his father and brother that he would not return to Alsace, neither would he go to the Polytechnique. They told him he must do

GUSTAVE DORE

either one or the other; and as the father was going back home in two days, Gustave could have just forty-eight hours in which to decide his destiny.

Passing by the office of the " Journal pour Rire," the father and son gaping in all the windows like true rustics, they saw announced an illustrated edition of " The Labors of Hercules." Some of the illustrations were shown in the window with the hope of tempting possible buyers. Gustave looked upon these illustrations with critical eye, and his face flushed scarlet—but he said nothing.

He knew the book; aye, every tale in it, with all its possible variations, had long been to him a bit of true history. To him Hercules lived yesterday, and, confusing hearsay with memory, he was almost ready to swear that he was present and used a shovel when the strong man cleaned the Augean stables.

The next morning, when his father and brother were ready to go to visit the Polytechnique, Gustave pleaded illness and was allowed to lie abed. But no sooner was he alone than he seized pencil and paper and began to make pictures illustrating " The Labors of Hercules."
¶ In two hours he had half a dozen pictures done, and fearing the return of his father he hurried with his pictures to Monsieur Philipon, director of the " Journal pour Rire." He shouldered past the attendants, pushed his way into the office of the great man, and spreading his pictures out on the desk cried, " Look here, sir!

GUSTAVE DORE

that is the way 'The Labors of Hercules' should be illustrated!"
It was the action of one absorbed and lost in an idea. Had he taken thought he would have hesitated, been abashed, self-conscious—and probably been repulsed by the flunkies—before seeing Monsieur Philipon. It was all the sublime effrontery and conceit—or naturalness, if you please—of a country bumpkin who did not know his place.
Philipon glanced at the pictures and then looked at the boy. Then he looked at the pictures. He called to another man in an adjoining room and they both looked at the pictures. Then they consulted in an undertone. It was suggested that the boy draw another illustration right there and then. They wished to make sure that he himself did the work, and they wanted to see how long it took ✽ ✽
Gustave sat down and drew another picture.
Philipon refused to let the lad leave the office, and dispatched a messenger for his father. When the father arrived, a contract was drawn up and signed, whereby it was provided that the "infant" should remain with Philipon for three years, on a yearly salary of five thousand francs, with the proviso that the lad should attend the school, Lycee Charlemagne, for four hours every day.
Thus, while yet a child, without discipline or the friendly instruction that wisdom might have lent, he

GUSTAVE DORE

was launched on the tossing tide of commercial life.
¶ His "Hercules" was immediately published and made a most decided hit—a palpable hit. Paris wanted more, and Philipon wished to supply the demand. The new artist's pictures in the "Journal pour Rire" boomed the circulation, and more illustrations were in demand. Philipon suggested that the four hours a day at school was unnecessary—Gustave knew more already than the teachers.

Gustave agreed with him, and his pay was doubled. More work rushed in, and Gustave illustrated serial after serial with ease and surety, giving to every picture a wildness and weirdness and awful comicality. The work was unlike anything ever before seen in Paris: every one was saying, "What next!" and to add to the interest, Philipon, from time to time, wrote articles for various publications concerning "the child illustrator" and "the artistic prodigy of the 'Journal pour Rire.'"
¶ With such an entree into life, how was it possible that he should ever become a master? His advantages were his disadvantages, and all his faults sprang naturally as a result of his marvelous genius. He was the victim of facility.

Everything in this world happens because something else has happened before. Had the thing that happened first been different, the thing that followed would not be what it is.

Had Gustave Dore entered the art world of Paris in the

GUSTAVE DORE

conventional way, the master might have toned down his exuberance, taught him reserve, and gradually led him along until his tastes were formed and character developed. And then, when he had found his gait and come to know his strength, the name of Paul Gustave Dore might have stood out alone as a bright star in the firmament—the one truly great modern.

Or, on the other hand, would the ossified discipline and set rules of a school have shamed him into smirking mediocrity and reduced his native genius to neutral salts?

Who will be presumptuous enough to say what would have occurred had not this happened and that first taken place?

GUSTAVE DORE

EFORE Gustave Dore had been in Paris a year his father died. Shortly after, the Strassburg home was broken up, and Madame Dore followed her son to Paris. Gustave's tireless pencil was bringing him a better income than his father had ever made; and the mother and three sons lived in comfort.

The mother admonished Gustave to apply himself to pure art, and not be influenced by Philipon and the others who were making fortunes by his genius. And this advice he intended to follow—not yet, but very soon. There were "Rabelais" and Balzac's "Contes Drolatiques" to illustrate. These done, he would then enter the atelier of one of the masters and take his time in doing the highest work.

But before the books were done, others came, with retainers in advance. Then a larger work was begun, to illustrate the Crimean War, in five hundred battle-scenes ❧ ❧

And so he worked—worked like a steam-engine—worked without ceasing. He illustrated Shakespeare's "Tempest" as only Dore could; then came Coleridge, Moore, Hood, Milton, Dante, Hugo, Gautier, and great plans were being laid to illustrate the Bible.

The years were slipping past. His brothers had found snug places in the army, and he and his mother lived together in affluence. Between them there was an affection that was very loverlike. They were comrades

GUSTAVE DORE

in everything—all his hopes, plans and ambitions were rehearsed to her. The love that he might have bestowed on a wife was reserved for his mother, and, fortunately, she had a mind strong enough to comprehend him.

In the corner of the large, sunny apartment that was set apart for his mother's room, he partitioned off a little room for himself, where he slept on an iron cot. He wished to be near her, so that each night he could tell her of what he had done during the day, and each morning rehearse his plans for the coming hours. By telling her, things shaped themselves, and as he described the pictures he would draw, others came to him

The confessional seems a crying need of every human heart—we wish to tell some one. And without this confessional, where one soul can outpour to another that fully sympathizes and understands, marriage is a hollow, whited mockery, full of dead men's bones

There is a desire of the heart that makes us long to impart our joy to another. Corot once caught the sunset on his canvas as the great orb sank, a golden ball, behind the hills of Barbizon. He wished to show the picture to some one—to tell some one, and looking around saw only a cottage on the edge of the wood a quarter of a mile away, and thither he ran, crying to the astonished farmer, " I 've got it! I 've got it! "

When Dore did a particularly good piece of work, in the first intoxication of joy he would run home, kiss his

GUSTAVE DORE

mother on both cheeks, and picking her up in his strong arms run with her about the rooms.

At other times he would play leap-frog over the chairs, vault over the piano, and jump across the table. And this wild joy that comes after work well done he knew for many years. In the evening, after a particularly good day, he would play the violin and sing entire scenes from some opera, his mother turning the leaves.

¶ As to his skill as a musician, is this testimonial on the back of a fine photograph I once had the pleasure of handling: " As a souvenir of tender friendship, presented to Gustave Dore, who joins with his genius as a painter the talents of a distinguished violinist and charming tenor.—G. Rossini."

The illustrations for Dante's " Inferno " were done in Dore's twenty-second year, and for this work he was decorated with the Cross of the Legion of Honor. He never did better work, and at this time his hand and brain seemed at their best.

Every great writer and every great artist makes vigorous use of his childhood impressions. Childhood does not know it is storing up for the days to come, but its memories sink deep into the soul, and when called upon to express, the man reaches out and prints from the plates that are bitten deep; and these are the pictures of his early youth—or else they tell of a time when he loved a woman.

The first named are the more reliable, for sex and love

GUSTAVE DORE

have been made forbidden subjects, until self-consciousness, affectation and untruth creep easily into their accounting. All literature and all art are secondary sex manifestations, just as surely as the song of birds or the color and perfume of flowers are sex qualities. And so it happens that all art and all literature is a confession; and it occurs, too, that childhood does not stand out sharp and clear on memory's chart until it is past and adolescence lies between. Then maturity gives back to the man the childhood that is gone forever. Many of the world's best specimens of literature are built on the impressions of childhood. Shakespeare, Victor Hugo, and I'll name you another—James Whitcomb Riley—have written immortal books with the autobiography of childhood for both warp and woof. Gustave Dore's best work is a reproduction of his childhood's thoughts, feelings and experiences—all well colored with the stuff that dreams are made of.

The background of every good Dore picture is a deep wood or mountain-pass or dark ravine. The wild, romantic passes of the Vosges, and the sullen crags, topped with dark mazes of wilderness, were ever in his mind, just as he saw them yesterday when he clutched his father's hand and held his breath to hear the singing of the wood-nymphs 'mong the branches.

His tracery of bark and branch, and drooping bough held down with weight of dew, are startlingly true. The great roots of giant trees, denuded by storm and flood,

GUSTAVE DORE

lie exposed to view; and deep vistas are given of shadowy glade and swift-running mountain torrent. All is somber, terrible, and tells of forces that tossed these mountain-tops like bowls, and of a Power immense, immeasurable, incomprehensible, eternal in the heavens.
¶ Dore's first exhibition in the Salon was made when he was eighteen, and a few years later, when he was presented with the Cross of the Legion of Honor, the decoration made his work exempt from jury examination. And so every year he sent some large painting to the Salon.

His work was the wonder of Paris, and on every hand his illustrations were in demand, but his canvases were too large in size and too terrible in subject to fit private residences.

Patrons were cautious.

To own a " Dore " was proof of a high appreciation of art, or else a lack of it—buyers did not know which. They were afraid of being laughed at.

His competitors began to hoot and jeer. Not being able to make pictures that would compete with his, they wrote him down in the magazines.

His name became a jest.

Various of his illustrations for the Bible were enlarged into immense canvases, some of which were twenty feet long and twelve feet high. All who looked upon these pictures were amazed by the fecundity in invention and the skill shown in drawing; but the most telling

GUSTAVE DORE

criticism against them was their defect in coloring. Dore could draw, but could not color, and the report was abroad that he was color-blind.

The only buyers for his pictures came from England and America. Paris loved art for art's sake, and the Bible was not popular enough to make its illustration worth while. " What is this book you are working on? " asked a caller

It was different in London, where Spurgeon preached every Sunday to three thousand people. The " Dores " taken to London attracted much attention—" mostly from the size of the canvases," Parisians said. But the particular subject was the real attraction. Instead of reading their daily " chapter," hard-working, tired people went to see a Dore Bible picture where it was exposed in some vacant storeroom and tuppence entrance-fee charged.

It occurred to certain capitalists that if people would go to see one Dore, why would not a Dore gallery pay?

A company was formed, agents were sent to Paris and negotiations begun. Finally, on payment of three hundred thousand dollars, forty large canvases were secured, with a promise of more to come.

Dore took the money, and, the agents being gone, ran home to tell his mother. She was at dinner with a little company of invited gests. Gustave vaulted over the piano, played leap-frog among the chairs, and turning a handspring across the table, incidentally sent his heels

GUSTAVE DORE

into a thousand-dollar chandelier that came toppling down, smashing every dish upon the table, and frightening the guests into hysterics.
"It's nothing," said Madame Dore; "it's nothing—Gustave has merely done a good day's work!"
The "Dore Gallery" in London proved a great success. Spurgeon advised his flock to see it, that they might the better comprehend Bible history; the Reverend Doctor Parker spoke of the painter as "one inspired by God"; Sunday-schools made excursions thither; men in hobnailed shoes knelt before the pictures, believing they were in the presence of a vision.
And all these things were duly advertised, just as we have been told of the old soldier who visited the Gettysburg Cyclorama at Chicago and looking upon the picture, he suddenly cried to his companion, "Down, Bill, down! by t' Lord, there's a feller sightin' his gun on us!"
Barnum offered the owners twice what they paid for the "Dore Gallery," with intent to move the pictures to America, but they were too wise to accept.
Twenty-eight of the canvases were eventually sold, however, for a sum greater than was paid for the lot, yet enough remained to make a most representative display; and no American in London misses seeing the Dore Gallery, any more than we omit Madame Tussaud's Wax-Works.
In Eighteen Hundred Seventy-three, Dore visited

GUSTAVE DORE

England and was welcomed as a conquering hero. The Prince of Wales and the nobility generally paid him every honor. He was presented to the Queen, and Victoria thanked him for the great work he had done, and asked him to inscribe for her a copy of the "Dore Bible."

More than this, the Queen directed that several Dore pictures be purchased and placed in Windsor Castle Of course, all Paris knew of Dore's success in England. Paris laughed. "What did I tell you?" said Berand. And Paris reasoned that what England and America gushed over must necessarily be very bad. The directors of the Salon made excuses for not hanging his pictures.

¶ Dore had become rich, but his own Paris—the Paris that had been a foster-mother to him—refused to accredit him the honor which he felt was his due.

In Eighteen Hundred Seventy-eight, smarting under the continued gibes and geers of artistic France, he modeled a statue which he entitled "Glory." It represents a woman holding fast in affectionate embrace a beautiful youth, whose name we are informed is Genius. The woman has in one hand a laurel-wreath; hidden in the leaves of this wreath is a dagger with which she is about to deal the victim a fatal blow.

Dore grew dispirited, and in vain did his mother and near friends seek to rally him out of the despondency that was settling down upon him. They said, "You are only a little over forty, and many a good man has never

GUSTAVE DORE

been recognized at all until after that—see Millet!"
¶ But he shook his head.
When his mother died, in Eighteen Hundred Eighty-one, it seemed to snap his last earthly tie. Of course he exaggerated the indifference there was towards him; he had many friends who loved him as a man and respected him as an artist.
But after the death of his mother he had nothing to live for, and thinking thus, he soon followed her.
He died in Eighteen Hundred Eighty-three, aged fifty years ✺ ✺

SO HERE ENDETH "LITTLE JOURNEYS TO THE HOMES OF EMINENT PAINTERS," WHICH IS VOLUME FOUR OF THE SERIES OF "LITTLE JOURNEYS TO THE HOMES OF THE GREAT," AS WRITTEN BY ELBERT HUBBARD. THE TYPOGRAPHY, BORDERS AND INITIALS WERE DESIGNED BY THE ROYCROFT ARTISTS AT THEIR SHOPS, WHICH ARE IN EAST AURORA, NEW YORK